Getting Past the Start

Becca Ramirez

WESTBOW
PRESS
A DIVISION OF THOMAS NELSON
& ZONDERVAN

Copyright © 2014 Rebecca Ramirez.

All rights reserved. No part of this book may be used or reproduced by any means, graphic, electronic, or mechanical, including photocopying, recording, taping or by any information storage retrieval system without the written permission of the publisher except in the case of brief quotations embodied in critical articles and reviews.

Unless otherwise noted, scripture taken from the Holy Bible, NEW INTERNATIONAL VERSION®. Copyright © 1973, 1978, 1984 by Biblica, Inc. All rights reserved worldwide. Used by permission. NEW INTERNATIONAL VERSION® and NIV® are registered trademarks of Biblica, Inc. Use of either trademark for the offering of goods or services requires the prior written consent of Biblica US, Inc.

Scripture quotations marked NKJV, taken from the New King James Version. Copyright © 1979, 1980, 1982 by Thomas Nelson, Inc. Used by permission. All rights reserved.

Scripture quotations marked ESV, are from The Holy Bible, English Standard Version® (ESV®), copyright © 2001 by Crossway, a publishing ministry of Good News Publishers. Used by permission. All rights reserved.

Scripture quotations marked MSG, are from The Message. Copyright © by Eugene H. Peterson 1993, 1994, 1995, 1996, 2000, 2001, 2002. Used by permission of NavPress Publishing Group.

WestBow Press books may be ordered through booksellers or by contacting:

WestBow Press
A Division of Thomas Nelson & Zondervan
1663 Liberty Drive
Bloomington, IN 47403
www.westbowpress.com
1 (866) 928-1240

Because of the dynamic nature of the Internet, any web addresses or links contained in this book may have changed since publication and may no longer be valid. The views expressed in this work are solely those of the author and do not necessarily reflect the views of the publisher, and the publisher hereby disclaims any responsibility for them.

Any people depicted in stock imagery provided by Thinkstock are models, and such images are being used for illustrative purposes only. Certain stock imagery © Thinkstock.

ISBN: 978-1-4908-5845-6 (sc)
ISBN: 978-1-4908-5846-3 (hc)
ISBN: 978-1-4908-5844-9 (e)

Library of Congress Control Number: 2014919503

Printed in the United States of America.

WestBow Press rev. date: 11/07/2014

Contents

Acknowledgments ix
Introduction xi
Chapter 1: At the Starting Line... 1
Chapter 2: When in Doubt, Start with Faith 13

Part 1: Spiritual Gifts 19
Chapter 3: First and Foremost, Salvation 21
Chapter 4: The Talent You Were Born With 32
Chapter 5: Holy Spirit Power 44
Chapter 6: Faith in the Spirit 52
Chapter 7: Reflections Stand Out from the Crowd 58

Part 2: God's Will, Not Mine 67
Chapter 8: Running with Direction 69
Chapter 9: An Eternal Focus 77
Chapter 10: Working toward a Perfect Reflection 83
Chapter 11: Live Like You Believe It 90
Chapter 12: Understanding His Will 98

Part 3: Service before Self 103
Chapter 13: Servant Leader 105
Chapter 14: Not a What But a Who 112
Chapter 15: Serving in the Day to Day 120

Part 4: On Your Mark ... Get Set ... Go! 127
Chapter 16: Well-Laid Plans to Rot 129
Chapter 17: Security in the Midst of Failure 141
Chapter 18: The Finish Line 148

Afterword 157
Bibliography 159
About the Author 163

To my precious girls,
Samara Jade and Aliyah Brielle,
I pray that you will always run with
God's purpose and direction.

Therefore, since we are surrounded by such a great cloud of witnesses, let us throw off everything that hinders and the sin that so easily entangles. And let us run with perseverance the race marked out for us, fixing our eyes on Jesus, the pioneer and perfecter of faith. For the joy set before him he endured the cross, scorning its shame, and sat down at the right hand of the throne of God.

—Hebrews 12:1–2

Acknowledgments

The process of writing this book was a long, wonderful, albeit somewhat arduous adventure. When I began, I had no idea what I was actually getting myself into, yet we find ourselves with a completed project that I am proud to call my first book. However, I would be remiss if I did not take the time to acknowledge the wonderful support that I have received along the way.

There is no way I could have done any of this without the incredible love and support of my family.

To my gracious husband, Kyle, thank you, thank you, thank you! Thank you for allowing me to take the time to escape into my writing and research. Thank you for being such an amazing father to our girls and taking on some extra work while I hashed out the final stages of the book. Thank you for always listening to my verbal process, even when you had no idea what on earth I was talking about. You are so good to me. I love you.

To my amazing parents, you have always been my loudest and most devoted cheerleaders. Thank you for encouraging me all along the way. Your belief in me allowed me the freedom to stretch my wings and jump, even if that meant failing and having to try again. So much of my success was built in the love and support that you consistently gave to me.

Thank you to my initial editing team. Judy and Stephanie. I am so grateful to count you as friends. The fact that you would be willing to take the time out of your lives to read my incredibly raw manuscript and give me honest criticism overwhelms my heart. I am indebted to you both.

I am obliged to Katie for being such an amazing inspiration to me. (I know you didn't believe I would actually include you. Now you are officially in my book. You're welcome.)

And last but certainly not least, to the amazing team at WestBow. You gave me a chance to fulfill my dream of truly becoming an author and not simply a writer who dreams. I am so humbled by the experience and the amount that you have taught me.

It is only by the grace of God, my Father, that any of this is possible.

Introduction

I love books that inspire change. It's not just about reading the words and going on with your life. Instead, it's about reading the words, allowing your soul to digest what they're saying, and giving the Spirit the freedom to move in your life and prompt change. Tom Stoppard says, "Words are sacred. They deserve respect. If you get the right ones, in the right order, you can nudge the world a little" (Stoppard 1982).

It is all too easy to read a good and inspiring book, feel the conviction from the first page to the last, and then set it aside with a simple "that was a good book" mentality and never change your direction.

Andy Stanley says, "Direction, not intention, determines your destination." (Stanley 2008)

I want to be a world changer. Not by myself, but I want to inspire others to join in and become world changers. It's not as impossible a dream as it may sound. We each have a unique circle of influence. Some people have a very small circle, whereas others have what seems like impossibly large circles. We aren't asked to change the world by ourselves. Rather we are called to spread the need for change to the people we know. We need to reach out to everyone we know and tell them about the life-changing love of Jesus and seek to serve as many people as we can. If we can inspire and ignite the initiative of the people within our circles of influence, then they can in turn spread that same inspiration to their circles and so on. This ripple effect can genuinely change lives and thus change the world.

I dream a lot. I like to imagine what it would be like to be a well-known author and be asked to speak at conferences, sharing the insights that God has given me. I imagine what it would be like to create a nonprofit organization to reach young ladies. I long to create an organization whose entire purpose is built around encouraging and inspiring teens in their faith and provide resources for them to achieve their dreams. As a mom, I imagine what my two young daughters will be like as they grow older. I imagine what the world will look like for this next generation, and that leads me to imagine what it will be like when Jesus comes back.

The world is quickly falling apart, and Christians speak against much of what is going on and how situations are being handled. But how much are we actually doing? We post quotes and statistics on our social media pages but rarely leave the comfort of our couches to actually do anything about whatever we are *standing* against. We're writing until our fingers develop calluses to inspire change, but if we don't start that change, how valuable are our words?

I am naturally an introvert. I like being around people I know and have relationships with. I like spending time with just my family but find it challenging to initiate a conversation with a group of people I don't know. I talk with people I already know and who already know me. I share my story with people who have either already heard it or who won't benefit from the wisdom I've learned from living it. What good does that do in regards to the kingdom?

God allows encouraging and challenging events to occur in our lives in order to guide us and to change us and to ultimately grow us. He is cultivating our lives to change His kingdom and to bring as many hearts to Him as we can prior to the second coming. He is allowing us time to reach out to more people. That is why Jesus hasn't come back yet. Our world is laden with atrocities and still we wait for His return. Think of the straight-up inhumanities that are occurring in our own backyards. What are we as Christians doing about it?

There is nothing wrong with appreciating the blessings that we have in life. But how are we affecting the lives of those around us? What are we *doing* to change the world for the better? Are we allowing God to take us on a journey that will allow Him to show the world all of His wonder and glory? Are we as believers really okay with staying in our comfort zones when God has clearly called us to so much more?

This is about change.

This book is about realizing the potential that God has placed inside each and every one of us and allowing Him to take control of that potential and making sure that change becomes a reality.

This is about getting out of the blocks and running the race before us rather than watching from the sidelines, which seems to have satisfied us up until now. This is about getting over the fear that has us paralyzed and recognizing that God will equip us to do all that we are called to do.

This is about getting past the start and finishing strong so that on that day when you are called home, you can stand before God and He can say, "Well done, good and faithful servant."

Upon the completion of each chapter you will find a chapter review. This will include the main focus points of the chapter as well as several questions. The questions are titled *Taking a Step over the starting line* because I believe that it is important to follow up on the proposed thoughts with practical application for our own lives.

I pray that as you read, you will find that God is speaking to you and calling you to step out in faith, fully believing that He will guide your every step.

CHAPTER 1

At the Starting Line

Imagine a track arena. There are metal bleachers encircling the sidelines, and the bleachers creak questionably as you walk across each row. Each step you take echoes with a clang in the open space below. As you look out from your view, you see the burnt red track lined in bright white paint. Then you see the horizontal line that designates the starting line. As you focus on that line, you notice people randomly appearing at that line. Some look confused and overwhelmed but cautiously take steps forward in their lanes. Others are eager and excited, bounding past the line and racing ahead as fast as they can.

As you look at each of the lanes, you notice that there are some who have fallen and appear to be injured and hurting. There are others who are still walking cautiously. It seems like they have barely moved forward at all. Still others are wandering from their lanes to other lanes, unable to find satisfaction with their current position. Everyone is at a different point. Everyone is going at different paces.

This is a picture of life. If you have yet to accept Jesus as your Savior, you are still in the bleachers, watching. There are others who may have made it down out of the stands but still remain on the sidelines, watching every move that each person makes in their races. Every step is critiqued. Every move or blunder is recorded. But if you have accepted Jesus as your Savior, then in that second, at that very moment when you say, "Yes, Jesus. I believe," you are transported from the sidelines to the starting line. You have your own lane. If you haven't figured it out yet, this isn't just life. This is your life. Everyone is running their own races, and you have to figure out how best to run yours. How do you proceed in order to finish well?

A person's life is often judged by his or her finish or final destination after years of hard work. We look at those who have *made it* with awe and admiration usually without taking the time to examine the process by which they got there or even considering what the process may have looked like. Our race should not be judged by others watching in the bleachers based on any one moment. It is a process that only one is positioned to judge, and thankfully that judge is known for His exceptional grace and mercy. Every other opinion just doesn't matter. They will judge. We claim that our inclination to judge one another is part of our human nature, though I think we use that as a crutch and a very sorry excuse. But to truly begin that process, we must first get started. It is that start that so often has us scared into either complacency or denial. What if I mess up? There is too much at stake. Will I even make it to the finish? And if I do, am I sure of where my final destination will be?

While I am emphasizing the race itself, this isn't to say that the destination isn't important. In all honesty our final destination is the most important thing we could ever contemplate. It's an eternal destination of pure joy and eternal union, or it's one of pure torture and separation from all that is good. But while we are on earth, what are our lives telling others about our destination? Can they tell if we are on the straight and narrow, staying true to the lane we are placed in, or do we blend into the seams of society, not allowing ourselves to be distinguishable to the passerby, aimlessly wandering into other people's lanes or off to the sidelines because they seem like they are more appealing?

It begins with understanding success. The world tries to indoctrinate us with a plethora of mentalities when it comes to being successful by its standards. "It's easy," people say. "It's simple really. All you have to do is—" Then they proceed to advise you about the *easy* steps that may or may not include selling both your soul and your firstborn.

These statements fill books of advice and dribble out of the mouths of speakers. We are pummeled with this mentality that we have to be good at everything. That is probably why we as a culture have accepted mediocrity as sufficient. If we have to be good at everything, we'd better lower the standards because otherwise we will make ourselves all a bunch of failures. And we can't possibly be failures. We're given this strange idea that in order to finish our race well, we have to be the best through our own strength and will, surpassing the standards that the world has placed on our lives.

Do you remember the time when people would get jobs and work for those companies for their entire lives? That was recipe for success in those days; however, if you are younger than twenty-five or thirty, you have probably never experienced it. You may have heard about Grandpa working for the same company from the day he got his first job as a teenager or straight out of high school until the day he retired. Now the average duration that workers, both hourly wage and salaried, have been with their current employer is 4.4 years. (Bureau of Labor Statistics 2010)[1] That is barely longer than it takes to graduate high school or earn a bachelor's degree. Twenty years ago that number was almost three times as much. (Bureau of Labor Statistics 2010)[2]

As a generation, we are filled with this "grass is greener" mentality. We may have decent jobs and pretty good benefits, but it's not good enough. It won't guarantee us the success that society tells us we need to ascertain. Perhaps you are still in school and you find that your parents are questioning and worrying about your ever-changing dreams and aspirations.

We are living in an age that puts a great deal of emphasis on finding the perfect job that is guaranteed to ensure the

---

[1] From January 2010, data included ages from sixteen through retirement age. The lowest duration was found in the twenty-five to thirty-four age range. http://www.bls.gov/opub/ted/2010/ted_20100927.htm

[2] From 1983 to 2000, the average tenure has fallen for men but has slightly increased for women though the tenure for women is still lower than that of men. Data collected from men and women aged thirty-five to fifty-four. http://www.bls.gov/opub/ted/2001/june/wk4/art05.htm

perfect life. Because of the cultural need to change jobs and positions so often, corporate companies are investing in applicants and paying for them to take the Myers-Briggs test or something similar to determine compatibility to the positions for which they are hiring. Students and employees alike are evaluating their personalities as well as their likes and dislikes. They are examining every aspect of who they are to decide what they should do with their lives. How can they ensure that success?

Christians have taken this same intense examining process and applied it to their spiritual lives. They take every test to reveal what their spiritual gifts might be. They evaluate their personalities to decide whether or not they are gifted to serve in particular capacities. We all evaluate our lives to see where on earth we could possibly fit in without ever stopping and taking the time to ask God where He is even placing us.

If you were to evaluate your life, what do you think you would find? Would you have a clear direction that you could venture into and feel successful at all levels of that decision? Or do you feel like you would be standing in the middle of a freeway, cars flying past you, all going somewhere when you can't seem to figure out how to even get going, let alone which way to turn once you've started?

Each day that we live, we take another step into our journey. We begin the day we're born. We may not realize it, but every detail adds up to create the people we are today and who we will be in the future, ranging from the friendships we create and either keep or dissolve to the foods we eat as we are raised and the importance we place on exercise and health. Little things—nothing that may seem to have any significance—can change our entire outlook on life and the journey that we are on.

There are a number of resources that list out individual steps to ensure both success and a purposeful life. Each one claims to give you the needed direction to fulfill the God-given calling on your life. But as much as we can appreciate those outlines and find peace in the assurances of clear direction, it still leaves us wondering, *What do I have that can be used to make a difference in the world? What makes me different from every other believer?*

Have you ever been stuck pondering those questions? Growing up, I was blessed to have parents who encouraged me to pursue all of the things my heart desired. I could do anything I set my mind to! So with that mentality, in just a few short years I pondered the possibility of becoming a biologist, a musician, a teacher, a biblical archeologist, a navigator for the US Navy, a lawyer, and even a lobbyist. I covered as many genres as possible during those four short years that comprised my high school experience. High school gave me the luxury of contemplating these dreams and aspirations; however, after I started college, I had to make a definitive decision. How on earth eighteen- or nineteen-year-old students are supposed to decide what they want to do for the rest of their lives is beyond me, but that is how our society has developed its system. Of the students I know in college, more than half of them have changed their majors at least once within the time they've spent working on their undergraduate degrees. Several of them changed their degrees three or four times before they settled on a specific focus.

We have this set idea that we need to know what is going to happen for the next forty or more years of our lives before we even know who we are and what we have been created to do. There are a number of good tools to get us focused on our spiritual mission, but at what point do we really know that *this* is what I was created for? We search for signs and directions that will indicate we are going in the right direction and pray that we will somehow lead successful lives.

While every person's specific calling from God is different, as our gifts and talents are different, God has not placed us on earth to wander around aimlessly. That does not mean that we are going to wake up on the day of our graduation and instantly know what specific jobs we are supposed to do to glorify God. My experience is a personal one, but it's one I wish to share with you. God's guidance and direction can always be found in different ways, but without a doubt, it is always found within His Word. Finding peace and direction through the Bible is a sure way to know that you are in line with God's will for your life, and it also helps give substantial assurance to the direction you feel Him calling you.

Finding your calling or direction is not an easy task. I know some people who are blessed to know without a shadow of doubt what they are supposed to do when they are still in their early twenties. I know others who have gone back and forth, always seeking God and His direction, but they still find themselves unsure of the definitive answer to their calling even into their forties and fifties ... and beyond.

God is interesting that way. We read that He speaks in the quiet and still times. But we also know that "as the heavens are higher than the earth, so are my ways higher than your ways and my thoughts than your thoughts" (Isaiah 55:9). In other words, when God gives us an answer, it is not always what we expect or want to hear.

Getting started is the hardest part. People commonly use different sports analogies, and "getting out of the blocks" for a race is a popular choice. Ask anyone who runs track, and they will tell you that the start, how people come off the blocks at the beginning of a race, can determine how well they will run that race. Of course, you will find exceptions to this as you do with anything. Some of the racers who face-plant at the start of the race are still able to get back up and finish strongly. But those who typically win the race usually have a smooth and swift start out of the blocks at the beginning.

Many times as I was trying to conceive what to write, I faced this dilemma. My mind told me, "It has already been written a thousand times. There is nothing that you can say that hasn't already been said ... and probably more eloquently that you could ever portray." More than anything I faced the lie of "you aren't good enough." We tear ourselves down before we even get started and never know what might have been, which is equivalent to succumbing to a glorious face-plant before even we start the race.

We are born with limitless amounts of potential. Unfortunately we have a propensity to become encumbered with too many wants and desires, unable to focus on any one thing. My parents once said, "We don't know what Becca could have done if she just carried it through. She could *do* a lot of things but hated practicing."

Unfortunately they were right. Whether it was art and piano lessons as a child or band and sports in high school, I always seemed to lack the self-motivational direction needed to greatly excel in any of the extracurricular activities that I filled my time with. The saddest reality of this saga is simply that I never really tried.

I was given every opportunity to be successful in a multitude of areas, but I didn't complete the work to bring it to fruition. Just as I was saying before, I had the "grass is greener" mentality. I hate to admit it, but I approached much of my education the same way.

We start projects (or sports or music classes or other activities), and though we enjoy them, we don't put our time and effort behind them. We sell ourselves short because we don't care enough or we just don't try hard enough. Then rather than accepting responsibility for the choices that led to our failures and disappointments, we put the blame solely on God.

What could have happened had I actually practiced my trumpet throughout high school? Or what colleges could I have been accepted into had I actually completed my homework and sought help for the subjects that plagued me and my grade point average? What if this apathy is the pattern in which I base my entire life? What if I were to approach ministry and my God-given calling the same way I approached playing the trumpet? Sure, I had some early success and showed some real talent, but I had better things to occupy my time as opposed to practicing. Why invest myself in something further than what is just on the surface? This is good enough, right? Besides, the grass is greener over here. Maybe I should try this instead. I'm sure to find greater success with this.

We get so focused on instantaneous success that we completely neglect the investment needed to truly succeed in something wonderful and great. If any amount of time and energy is required beyond the initial exertion, we look for an opportunity to move on to the next thing that is sure to be better.

Just as I started my plethora of activities and never saw them through to completion, perhaps you find yourself in the same situation without even realizing how much more God has in store for you.

Here's the thing. We are so much more than simply what we do. Our success is found in who God says that we are and ultimately that success is seen as we bring God glory through our lives. What we do is relative, but how we live can be seen as a determinate of our success.

It's pretty easy to spot that there is a vast divide between the world's standards of success and God's standards of success. As believers, we are seeking enough faith so that we can cast aside the world's ideas and live completely and confidently within God's ideas. But we must be cautious to remember that our faith is not tied to doing good works.

Are we so focused on "doing good" that we forget to do what God is asking us to do? Are our actions, either in our career or in our personal lives, bringing people closer to knowing God and His wonders, or are they alienating them further? We are given a number of tools to accomplish everything that is asked of us. It won't always feel that we are adequately equipped, but that is where true faith sets in.

The wonderful news for all of us is that there isn't a singular moment that will define success or failure within our race. In the process of running our race, we will find a plethora of options. Those options could all be viable choices in what God wants us to do. Take comfort in the truth that the only *wrong* choice is to not run your race or to walk away from it. We are all here for a reason, and we will all fulfill that reason by the grace of God alone.

Chapter 1 Review

Focus points

- The world's definition of success does not equal God's definition of success.
- Choosing the *wrong path* will not derail your ability to fulfill God's purpose for your life.
- God's definition of success requires an investment of time, energy, and obedience, not just good works.
- What we do is relative, but how we live can be seen as a determinate of our success.

Taking a Step over the starting line

- How would you define success?
- Does it line up closer to the world's definition or with God's?
- Do you have a tendency to start projects but never finish them?
- How can you refocus your priorities so that does not become a pattern by which you live?

CHAPTER 2

When in Doubt, Start with Faith

We are all uniquely created to do *something* great for the kingdom of God. Doesn't that feel like such a daunting task? I have to admit that when I stop and think about my life directly relating to giving the Creator of the universe glory and honor, I become timid. Am I doing the right thing? Am I making good decisions? How badly can I mess this up and still give God glory? These questions may be pointless to ask, but there is a deep stream of meaning that we can find when we are able to come to a solid conclusion on all of them. As long as I am seeking after God, He will guide me no matter how much I mess up. The end of the story is already written, and God gets the glory. In other words, it is not our ability but rather our availability that will lead to success.

No matter what you or I do, in the end God will be glorified. We just get the privilege of being a part of it. Proverbs tells us, "Trust in the Lord with all your heart and lean not on your own understandings. But in all your ways acknowledge him, and he shall direct your paths" (Proverbs 3:5–6 NKJV).

That was my favorite verse growing up. While part of it had to do with the fact that it was one of the first ones I was able to actually memorize, I found myself coming back to it time and time again. There was truth in those words, and at every turning point when I had no idea what was going on, trusting in God gave me a starting point to work from. Then once I was able to grasp ahold of that, I was able to start moving forward.

The challenge is reaching a point when we can trust ourselves to differentiate between when to stay still and when to move forward. We praise the faith of those who step out into the great unknown, but we likewise honor those who "wait patiently on the Lord" sometimes for years and years. Abraham is a great example of both instances.

In Genesis 12, we find Abraham (at this point still known as Abram) receiving the call from the Lord.

> The LORD had said to Abram, "Go from your country, your people and your father's household to the land I will show you.
> "I will make you into a great nation, and I will bless you; I will make your name great, and you will be a blessing. I will bless those who bless you, and whoever curses you I will curse; and all peoples on earth will be blessed through you."
> So Abram went, as the LORD had told him." (Genesis 12:1–4)

It doesn't say that Abraham had to think about it and get everything situated before he was able to leave the land he was born and raised in and had always known. There is no record of him packing everything up or waiting until the tent could be sold. It doesn't say that he even knew where he was going. It simply says that he went.

And in even greater faith he went while he believed in a seemingly impossible promise made by God. God had told Abraham that He would make him into a great nation. For this to come to fruition he had to first have children. We are introduced to his wife, Sarah (Sarai), at the beginning of the chapter by being told that she is barren and therefore childless. To the finite mind, how can a woman who is barren have a legacy that will be as numerous as the stars in the sky (Genesis 15:5)? This was obviously something that Abraham also struggled to understand and thus tried to bring about his legacy on his own by having a son with one of his servants.

Our understanding is so limited. When we don't understand, we are convinced that we have to do something to make it all come together. But God comes and tells Abraham that he will indeed have a son by his wife and that this son will be his heir. It wasn't about Abraham doing the right thing. It was about him believing that God would do what He said He would do. And then comes one of my favorite verses. "Abram believed the LORD, and he credited it to him as righteousness" (Genesis 15:6).

Abraham had to wait to see the fulfillment of God's promise and his purpose. And because he believed, God called him righteous.

During this waiting period Abraham and God weren't just sitting there, twiddling their thumbs, waiting for the cosmic powers to line up at precisely the right moment for God to perform the miracle necessary to fulfill His promise. God was refining Abraham's faith through endurance. It's one of the reasons patience is defined as long-suffering. It is rarely enjoyable but oftentimes necessary for us to come to a place that we will have the faith necessary to do all that God wants us to do.

I don't know of any foolproof manner to determine if you are in a time of waiting or of stepping out in blind faith. However, I do know that our purpose is not one singular, all-powerful, life-changing moment, and if we happen to miss that hypothetical moment, the world won't implode. You see, I have this theory. What if there isn't just one thing that we are supposed to do in life? Or … what if our purpose is not simply what we do but who we impact? How would that change our approach to life as a whole?

As I read Scripture, I see several areas that can be combined together to give direction to our ultimate purpose. Like I said, there unfortunately isn't some grandiose equation that you can put specific activities into, add a generic amount of time, and pop out a God-approved plan for your life, but there are several areas that can give you the confident assurance to trust God as you step out in your journey. They are comprised of spiritual gifts, submitting to God's will over your own, serving selflessly, and finally getting up and moving forward.

While we may be scared of messing up God's grand design because we can't figure out what our purpose is supposed to be, the truth is that we can't. We simply are not powerful enough to throw a wrench in God's plans. No matter what we do, God loves us. He loves us with such a perfect and sacrificial love that He sent Jesus to earth to ultimately die on the cross for our sins. He also loves us so much that He overcame death and rose from the grave after three days to show that He was in fact victorious and all that He claimed to be. And He wants to share that same victory with each and every one of us. It is the message of the cross that compels us to serve. It is that assurance of the salvation that pushes us to be more than we can ever be on our own. It is because of the cross and the resurrection that we are blessed with spiritual gifts to serve others and ultimately glorify God. That is the point. That is why we are here. And that is why we continue to search for the answers to get us past the start and ultimately across the finish line.

Chapter 2 Review

Focus points

- Faith is monumental for a successful race.
- Success is rarely instantaneous.
- No matter what we do, God will be glorified!

Taking a Step over the starting line

- Becca mentioned that God used a waiting period to refine and grow Abraham's faith. Have you experienced a time when you felt like you were in the midst of a waiting period?
- How did that time cause your faith to grow and mature?
- If you currently find yourself in a time of waiting, what are three things you can actively do to continue seeking God and to foster your faith?

Part 1
Spiritual Gifts

CHAPTER 3

First and Foremost, Salvation

The Holy Spirit gets the short end of the stick more often than not from a lot of people (and churches). For a time I attended a common denominational church that was a truly God-fearing church. It was a solid church that helped me learn about God's sacrifice and love. But I cannot remember a single Sunday when the Holy Spirit was mentioned more than simply a reference during a reading or benediction. There was never a sermon that spoke into His amazing characteristics and why He is a part of the Trinity.

Among different denominations there are a multitude of different beliefs surrounding the Holy Spirit. For example, the Southern Baptists traditionally believe what is called a cessationist doctrine. This particular viewpoint believes that the gifts of the Spirit are not operational in the church today, especially tongues and prophecy. (von Buseck 2014) In the Catholic church, however, the standing according to the *Catholic Encyclopedia* is that the Holy Spirit precedes the Father and the Son and that the gifts are "first specially intended for the sanctification of the person who receives them" and second is "extraordinary favors granted for the help of others" (charismata). (Forget 1910) It is important to state that this is not an across-the-board statement for any one denomination. Different people and churches within these denominations will hold different beliefs.

While I believe some viewpoints are debatable, what absolutely cannot be debated is that the Holy Spirit is as much God as the Father and as Jesus. He also happens to be the most mysterious. We can't seem to wrap our heads around the "nonphysical but always with us" notion that He encompasses. Yet Jesus told the disciples that it was *better* that He leave them because something better was coming in His place.

> But now I am going to him who sent me. None of you asks me, "Where are you going?" Rather, you are filled with grief because I have said these things. But very truly I tell you, it is for your good that I am going away. Unless I go away, the Advocate will not come to you; but if I go, I will send him to you. When he comes, he will prove the world to be in the wrong about sin and righteousness and judgment: about sin, because people do not believe in me; about righteousness, because I am going to the Father, where you can see me no longer; and about judgment, because the prince of this world now stands condemned. (John 16:5–11)

The Holy Spirit is what came in place of Jesus. Not only is He as much God as Jesus is, but He can be everywhere as a part of each of us all at the same time. A physical being simply cannot accomplish this feat. If we have accepted Jesus as our Savior and confessed our sins to God, then the Bible is clear that we have the Holy Spirit dwelling within us. He is there to guide us and direct us, but with His indwelling we also have claim to what are called spiritual gifts.

Spiritual gifts are discussed and listed several places in the New Testament, including 1 Corinthians 12, Ephesians 4, Romans 12, and 1 Peter 4. There are also other gifts mentioned throughout Scripture that are often filed under the "God-given talents" category. Some of the additional gifts include areas such as music or leadership. There are those who will debate gifts versus talents, but that is not my focus. I believe that there are some points that Scripture describes that are not painted as black and white, and there are some points that are abundantly black and white. The gifts of the Spirit and the division of what those gifts are called, how they are *given*, and what exactly those gifts are can be interpreted in a number of ways. Ultimately there are three main gifts discussed—eternal life, natural gifts (talents), and spiritual gifts.

I want to take the time to discuss each of these three areas. My prayer and hope is that I am able to clear up any of the major discrepancies preventing you from understanding and utilizing these amazing and powerful gifts.

The first gift given to us is eternal life. As believers, we receive this gift of life when we accept Jesus as our Savior. Romans 6:23 (ESV) says, "For the wages of sin is death, but the *free gift* of God is eternal life in Christ Jesus our Lord" (emphasis mine). Similarly John 1:12 (ESV) says, "But to all who did receive him, who believed in his name, he gave the right to become children of God."

There is no denying that this is in fact a gift. It is a wonderful and humbling gift of grace. Grace is described as undeserved favor. We do absolutely nothing to deserve it, and in fact, we truly deserve a wretched and abandoned eternity because even on our greatest days in our finest moments, the best that we can accomplish through our own merit falls painfully short of righteous perfection. I know that even on my best day I will leave a pile of dishes in the sink for my husband to wash because I'm feeling lazy and I just honestly do not like washing dishes. On my best days I will still think sarcastic and genuinely unkind thoughts about the guy who cut me off in traffic. On my best days I am still foolish, disobedient, and a slave to my various passions and desires. This is what it says in Titus.

> For we ourselves were once foolish, disobedient, led astray, slaves to various passions and pleasures, passing our days in malice and envy, hated by others and hating one another. But when the goodness and loving kindness of God our Savior appeared, he saved us, not because of works done by us in righteousness, but according to his own mercy, by the washing of regeneration and renewal of the Holy Spirit, whom he poured out on us richly through Jesus Christ our Savior, so that being justified by his grace we might

become heirs according to the hope of eternal life. (Titus 3:3–7 ESV)

I love that "he saved us not because of works done by us in righteousness, but according to his own mercy ... so that being justified by his grace we might become heirs according to the hope of eternal life." I mean, really, I'm knocked off my feet in humility at those words, at that promise. Nothing I do is going to get me into heaven. It was entirely done according to *His own mercy.* Wow!

Words are so incredible, and how they are used can be powerful. This is a case of that beautiful combination of words that can strike right to the heart of a matter. I like looking up words in the dictionary. Okay, I like looking up words on dictionary.com. I do think I still own a real, paperbound dictionary that weighs about as much as my youngest daughter, but the convenience of popping around the online version is hard to beat. But going back to my point, I love looking up words, even the ones of which I know the definitions, mostly because I enjoy finding the idiosyncrasies of how and when certain words are used. I did this for mercy. I know that benevolence is a common synonym, but I had another humbling moment when I read the first definition listed. "Compassion or kindly forbearance shown toward an offender, an enemy, or other person in one's power."

There is a political phrase that is used for those people who are considered an extreme threat to national security. It is "enemy of the state." It was also a really good thriller movie starring Will Smith. But that's only slightly relevant to this. You see, the idea of an enemy of the state is that you are on the country's official hit list. It's based on the idea that you have done something egregious enough that officials are going to invest a significant amount of man power and money to rid themselves of you.

We are enemies of the state to God. Our sins are egregious enough that we cannot make amends on our own. All of our strengths and goodwill are not enough to change the opinion of our eternal sentence. As we read about the hopelessness of our situation, we find one tiny three-letter word that is beautiful and powerful in its incredible simplicity, capable of changing the direction of a sentence—the word *but*. Whenever the Bible uses *but* after it describes our condemning evidence against God, it's a sign of His mercy. It's proof that He loves us so desperately that He did everything necessary to ensure that we had a gift of mercy. We are enemies of God, *but* Jesus extended us mercy. And through that mercy we are gifted an inheritance of heaven itself.

Because of this incredible gift of salvation through mercy, we are adopted into God's family.

The print media loves to emphasize the differentiation between biological and adopted children. For example, whenever a magazine writes anything about Angelina Jolie and her children, they take the time and print space to make the distinction between the children she adopted and the children she gave birth to. But if you were to ask any parent who has the honor of having both adopted children and biological children, they will tell you that all of the kids are simply their children. To parents who love their children, there is no difference in love between the ones who share their genes and the ones who don't. They are all blessings and equal members of their families.

This is the same for God. When Scripture tells us that we have been adopted into the kingdom, it is not a second-class tier. We are all heirs to the kingdom equally. It doesn't matter that we aren't there by our own merit. It doesn't matter that we are only there because of an incredible gift of mercy. We are as much a member of God's family as anyone else because He chose to extend that amazing grace to us and adopt us as His own.

You might be wondering why I'm even bothering to go over this. The likelihood is that if you are seeking God's purpose in your life, you already have some sort of relationship with Him. Perhaps, but let me say this plainly because you are going to hear me say it several times before we are done. If you don't get this gift, the other two don't matter. If you don't grasp the magnitude that comes with accepting the gift of eternal life, then how you live your life, purposeful or not, really won't matter much in the end. It may make you feel better about yourself, but it won't change your eternal destination. This free gift of life is talking about our eternal souls, but it is also telling us who we are. Read John 1:12 again. "But to all who did receive him. Who believed in his name, he gave the right to become children of God."

With this gift of life we are now part of the family. Have you ever noticed how you act differently around your family than you do around strangers? I know that I am more relaxed. I speak freely, knowing that I am around people who love me. I act more intentionally because I am around people I care about and because I want the best for them. Likewise, as a child of God, I am able to approach the throne of the Creator of the universe and come to Him like I would my father. I respect Him, but I am also able to crawl into His lap and allow Him to just hold me tight when I need to be comforted. In the same way I am more intentional in loving my family, I am more intentional about serving and loving God and His people (the church) and reaching out to those who are not yet part of the family because I know that God's desire is that everyone be saved and redeemed.

This gift of eternal life is so important that people die for it on a regular basis. Martyrs of the Christian faith give their lives willingly so that others might have even the opportunity to just hear the truths that have so desperately changed their own lives.

The power that lies in the name of Jesus is tremendous. His name alone scares the demons that Satan has doing his bidding around the world. The reason why other religions are threatened by Christianity is because of that name. They try to say we need to just coexist. They claim that Christians are intolerant. And truthfully some Christians are intolerant to other beliefs, and we do need to live as peacefully as possible with everyone no matter what they believe; however, there is one thing that we as Christians cannot waver on. We can never deny the fact that Jesus told us that there is only one way to get to heaven. It's not a negotiation. It's not some debate that we need to have in order to come to a point that we can agree on. C. S. Lewis said it best in his book *Mere Christianity* when he said,

> I am trying here to prevent anyone saying the really foolish thing that people often say about Him: "I'm ready to accept Jesus as a great moral teacher, but I don't accept His claim to be God." That is the one thing we must not say. A man who said the sort of things Jesus said would not be a great moral teacher. He would either be a lunatic—on a level with the man who says he is a poached egg—or else he would be the Devil of Hell. You must make your choice. Either this man was, and is, the Son of God: or else a madman or something worse. You can shut Him up for a fool, you can spit at Him and kill Him as a demon; or you can fall at His feet and call Him Lord and God. But let us not come with any patronizing nonsense about His being a great human teacher. He has not left that open to us. He did not intend to. (Lewis 1952)

The entire reason that Jesus came to earth, lived the way He did, and died the way He did was so that we could be made righteous. It was so that we could have mercy extended to us in the first place. It was so we could be brought into God's family as His children. We can't do it on our own. We cannot be good enough. If you have any doubts about that one fact, read through the Jewish law and tell me if you can maintain that kind of purity. I can't. The exclusion of bacon alone would knock me out of perfection, let alone the actual serious stuff.

But because God is good, not like the human standard of good but the awesome and beyond compare actual definition of good, He made a way. Jesus didn't just die, but He came back to life to show that He conquered death, and that is our ticket to heaven. That is our gift of eternal life. Because I trust and serve a God who is stronger than death itself, I, too, am gifted eternal life with Him, through Him, and by His incomparable mercy.

Chapter 3 Review

Focus points

- The Holy Spirit is absolutely vital to our success.
- The Holy Spirit gives us three distinct gifts—salvation, talents, and spiritual gifts.
- Grace is by far the greatest gift we could ever receive.
- We are saved only by mercy, and it is through this mercy that we become part of God's family and thus heirs to the kingdom of heaven.

Taking a Step over the starting line

- What does it mean to be an enemy of the state toward God?
- What does it mean to be an heir to the kingdom of God?
- How does God's mercy take us from being enemies of the state to heirs?

Chapter 4

The Talent You Were Born With

The second gifts talked about in Scripture are those natural gifts or those talents we are born with. To help identify your natural gifts, think through what you are *good* at and the things that you enjoy. Are you a natural-born organizer and find yourself distracted by the details, especially if someone did not pay any heed to them? Do you find yourself naturally taking charge and mentoring others? No matter what you find pleasure in, the Holy Spirit has gifted you uniquely to fulfill your God-given calling … and often in ways that we are already naturally inclined to do.

I am taking the liberty of calling these talents gifts for a couple of reasons. The reality that God has created each and every one of us in a specifically unique manner is more than simply a talent. It is a gift. Are they gifts that require having a relationship with Holy Spirit as a prerequisite? No, there are millions of people throughout the world who are insurmountably talented in one facet or another and yet have no semblance of even acknowledging God as their Creator, let alone their Savior.

But there is something so humbling about recognizing that you have a talent and then realizing that you can use that talent to honor God.

If you still doubt my categorization, I want to challenge you. Who are your favorite musicians? Have you ever heard a piece of music and felt your heart tighten or tears well in your eyes from emotion that came out of seemingly nowhere? Or look at the great masterpieces that line the walls of museums around the world. Look to the creations that men have put on a piece of canvas or created out of metal or stone. Expressing the grandeur of God is not something that is limited to the Bible. He shows Himself through these talents. He shows the creativity that He used to compose the symphony of the stars through the musical talents of composers who script notes together in beautifully complex harmonies. He paints the skies with the most glorious colors every morning and every night, giving inspiration to those who attempt to capture that beauty on film or through paints.

Not every person with talents uses them for God's glory, but they have the opportunity to do just that. Some of the most powerful, life-changing stories are ones that show someone who is talented but lost finding Jesus and then turning around and using that talent to bring others into the kingdom as well. That is truly a gift.

While I was working with the youth at church, I was given a number of opportunities to meet a complete conglomeration of people—all ages, all races, all socioeconomic backgrounds.

It didn't matter who they are or where they've come from. The church found a way to love them and to bring them into the fold. It was such a refreshing example of what it looks like to love the person but not the sin.

As I was writing this section, I knew I wanted to include a personal testimony that spoke right to the heart of the matter, that pierced this idea that we can find our own way, but unless we trust God to lead us, we will fall down farther than we could imagine. I wanted to find a way to paint the picture of someone who had raw talent but was lost without the guidance from God. The person that came to mind was Damien.

When I first met Damien, he was still new to the faith. I heard him perform a spoken word piece that astonished me at the depth and maturity that filled his poetry. Every time I saw him, he had a smile on his face and genuine joy in his heart. It wasn't a fake smile you'd put on because you are at church, but it was the look that encompassed true joy that could only come from knowing God's true, unfathomable grace.

When I first considered how to best write this, I automatically assumed I would summarize his testimony. I assumed I would put my spin on the effect that God had on using his talents for the kingdom. But the more I reflected on what God wanted to say, the more I knew it would have to be communicated in His own words. So I asked Damien to write out his testimony for me. And even without any direction from me, he did in the form that he does best, poetry. He wrote the words and the format in the style in which he would speak it, and so I want to share that with you verbatim just as he shared it with me. He included the following advice with the transcript: As you are reading, if there is any doubt on how to read it, read it phonetically. I also recommend reading it out loud to fully grasp the beauty of his words.

> As long as I have your attention,
>
> Allow me to slip into and break the tension—that silence creates when people start to listen—attentively,
>
> Take a deep breath with me and—(inhale) the smoke of past memories and reminisce with me in this moment,
>
> See it was only—four years ago that if you had asked me who I be—I would have recited my blood creed,
>
> More or less I be that bloody Damien—that goony goon goo,
>
> Bangin for nine-trey gangstaz aka NTG,
>
> I bang that five for the spiritually, physically, mentally, and economically,
>
> I be that triple O gangsta ride-bangin for OG Tye—cut a crab eat a crab,
>
> Suwoop poppin—slow for those who oppose against my nation,

Lock and load—rep for the east side,

Rest in Peace to my OG Tye—snake eye red, 50/50 love all dogs bang for blood,

And I was a blood banga indeed, I was a gang member at the age of 16 and had ever felt more G,

See growing up I was always warned about the gang life,

But no one ever sat me down and told me how shiny and attractive the gang life might sound,

See I felt like a nobody—an island claimed by no country,

I was alone so you know I was never rightly fed—so I was only left hungry,

But I was—hungry for a meaning – meaning I never saw in my eyes a purpose that was actually worth it,

Something I could live for—fight for—or die for,

And now all these grown men are asking me who imma bang for,

So I picked up my red bandana and sought the approval of my fellow gang members—I—was no longer an island,

Getting Past the Start

But now I was a part of something bigger—than myself, but now I valued a color so that I could find value in self—and,

I was content for a short while, but while I gave in to peer pressure the pressure began to press down on my mentality,

And it was shortly after this that I began to see that I would soon be the cause of my own fatality,

See I held this high image that boys would always have my back—blood in blood out and we would always be family,

But it's funny that if my—real blood ain't in them then my blood members would be out faster than the blood cells out my body when I receive a cut- on my hand—see,

I was an island—that was finally claimed by a country but when it came down to—real war—it was alone. I. stand.

Because the only road in which I was standing was so broad I could get lost and nobody would ever notice I was gone,

And this—angered my soul—because this meant I made these gang members my king,

But Jesus shortly reminded me that He played this game some time ago and He got the ruler of this world on check-mate,

Meaning I no longer had to check my fate at the door—but now I'm—free to live a life—free of underlying deceit,

No longer being discreet—about my actions—but living free—in satisfaction in the purpose God has given me,

See Christ raised me from my grave-site,

And He placed me in the same light Saul stood when he turned into Paul and he waited three days so that He could see again,

It was those same eyes God gave Paul to see that as soon as I surrendered to Him he gave me and,

There was a blood transfusion that took place,

I no longer lived—for a blood gang— But now I lived—because the blood came,

For me—Christ died on a tree—and His body was ripped for all to see,

And his blood bled—til He was dead—and he rose again just to prove He was—who he once said,

So now I stand here before you—washed clean by His blood,

And now I stand here before you drenched in His love,

And now I stand here before you to tell you—He's enough,

Christ didn't die so that we could live lives separated from Him,

He died so that we could stand here and say – I am blood certified.

Damien has since graduated college with a degree in Christian ministry and is working on a church staff as a youth leader.

There is nothing that can't be redeemed for the glory of God—whether it's turning a gang member into a youth pastor and incredibly gifted poet or turning the sports world on its head by inserting true and undeniably outspoken believers on the television sets of people worldwide on a weekly basis.

It is nearly impossible to watch a football game where one of the players, upon scoring a touchdown, does not either point to heaven or take a knee for a moment of thanks. I had the privilege of being a student at the University of Florida when the Gators won three national championships in two years (one football championship in 2006, two basketball championships in 2006 and 2007). I was also lucky enough to find myself in the crowd at the 2008 NCAA Football National Championship when the Gators beat the Oklahoma Sooners 24–14. During the glory years at the University of Florida, a tremendous amount of press was dedicated to the football quarterback, Tim Tebow. Tim Tebow is an outspoken Christian who dedicated everything he did, whether he was playing football or serving in the Philippines with his family, to the glory of God. This included his football success. By the end of his senior year at Florida, there were as many people who loved him for his faith as those who despised him for it. Some assumed that it was false humility and tried to pinpoint each and every flaw that he had. They questioned him on his motives for wanting to focus on football if he loved God so much. More often than not, Tebow would just smile, respond to criticism with more grace than I could ever muster, and tell everyone that Jesus was his number-one priority and that football was also a priority but was never above Jesus.

Eric Liddell, an Olympian runner, also knew a thing or two about the pressure of balancing his love and devotion to his faith and to his sport. While it's said that this is not an actual quote from Liddell, *Chariots of Fire* (a movie based around Liddell) quotes him as saying, "I believe God made me for a purpose, but he also made me fast. And when I run, I feel his pleasure." (Hudson 1981)

People like Eric Liddell or Tim Tebow have been gifted in sports and agility. They have taken this gift and turned it back around to give God the glory. Damien was gifted with a talent in poetry and a heart that wanted to belong. God took his heart and turned it in tune with His own, claiming him as part of His family, giving him a place to thrive. When we are able to focus our hearts on God and the advancement of His kingdom, we do not have to stress about our own self-worth. It is not about building me up or about how good I feel. It is about doing those things I find myself talented in … and doing them to the best of my ability because God gave me those talents to bring glory to His kingdom.

The Bible supports this premise as well. Depending on the people you talk to and their backgrounds, names and titles can change for these particular gifts. In Ephesians 4, it lists some of these ministry gifts or specific gifts and talents given to further the kingdom and expand the church body. "So Christ himself gave the apostles, the prophets, the evangelists, the shepherds, and teachers, to equip his people for the work of service, so that the body of Christ might be built up" (Ephesians 4:11–12).

The Bible doesn't necessarily tell us how these roles look or how they are specifically played out. In the same way that different people learn in different manners, these roles can look different depending on who God is reaching in that moment.

Talents are given to us for the ultimate purpose of serving God through them. They are the unique parts of ourselves that we often use in claiming our identities. And our identities will ultimately determine the decisions we make.

During the summer of 2013, I had the opportunity to go on a mission trip to Romania. The focus of our outreach was to the Roma (gypsy) children. In a country that has made strides to step into equal light with other European nations, there is still drastic racial tension toward this particular people.

Our team took the time to study Ruth while we were there to see and understand the love that God has for *outsiders*. The identity of Ruth is pretty phenomenal. She wasn't an Israelite. She was a Moabite (in short, not one of God's chosen people). She was a widow without a son to carry on the family legacy. She was an outsider in Judah. But despite everything that was seemingly stacked against her, she was chosen because she found her identity in the God of Israel. "Your people will be my people and your God my God" (Ruth 1:16).

Talents or ministry gifts are vital to who we are as individuals and who we are within the church. They help us to relate to some people and set us apart from others. They bring us joy and help us grow in our understanding of who God is so that we can better find our ultimate identity in Him. While they are not gifts that require a relationship with Jesus, we will never truly experience the depth of their greatness without the knowledge and understanding of where they came from in the first place.

Chapter 4 Review

Focus points

- Your talents are gifts from God.
- While we may be talented whether or not we believe in God, our talents were designed to glorify Him.
- Our talents are parts of our identities.
- We have different talents, and thus, we are be able to serve God in different manners.

Taking a Step over the starting line

- What talents do you have?
- How can you utilize them to glorify God?

CHAPTER 5

Holy Spirit Power

The third type of gifts that God gives us is what we typically understand as spiritual gifts through the Holy Spirit.

Now I must admit that I feel inadequate to write on this particular area. It intimidates me for so many reasons. Despite that, I feel as though God is calling me to write this section with the confidence and assurance of His guidance.

The main distinction between what we understand as spiritual gifts versus those we just discussed as talents and ministry gifts is the manifestation of the Spirit. In other words, if you are doing the work by your own strength or skill, it would not be classified as an instance of the power of the spiritual gifts.

In 1 Corinthians 12:1, Paul is speaking directly to the church of Corinth (and to us today) as he says, "Now about spiritual gifts, brothers, I do not want you to be ignorant." He goes on to list them but not before he emphasizes that "there are different kinds of gifts, but the same Spirit."

He says something similar to the church of Ephesus. "There is one body and one Spirit—just as you were called to hope when you were called—one Lord, one faith, one baptism; one God and Father of all, who is over all and through all and in all. But to each one of us grace has been given as Christ apportioned it" (Ephesians 4:4–7).

This leads me to understand that the gifts of the Spirit are as He chooses to bestow them for the edification and expansion of the church. I love that after he lists several examples of what some of the gifts are, he concludes with their sole purpose, which we can likewise understand as our main purpose "to prepare God's people for works of service, so that the body of Christ may be built up until we all reach unity in the faith and in the knowledge of the Son of God and become mature, attaining to the whole measure of the fullness of Christ" (Ephesians 4:12–13).

This idea was not singularly accredited to Paul. In 1 Peter 4:10, we find that Peter supports this same mentality when he says, "Each one should use whatever gift he has received to serve others, faithfully administering God's grace in its various forms."

The gifts of the Spirit are to get people's attention. Think of them like the obnoxiously bright flashing signs on the side of the road while you are driving at night. There is no excuse for not seeing them. Howard Carter said during a question-and-answer forum that the gifts of the Spirit are for signs to capture our attention and to see the mighty hand of God. (Carter 1991) God wants to show Himself to each and every one of us. He wants us to know His might as well as His mercy.

There are many explanations on the gifts themselves and what order we should "covet them" (referring to 1 Corinthians 12:31). One side will tell us that we each are given one main gift (giving the reasoning behind the desire to take a spiritual gifts test, which many churches support). Then on the other end of the spectrum, there are explanations that tell us we are capable (and should desire) to be given each and every gift. Because of the extreme differences, I will not take a stance. I do this partially because I simply do not know and mainly because I cannot scripturally determine the necessity in doing so.

I have grown up understanding spiritual gifts as one thing and continue to see the perspective of spiritual gifts being something else. I see in Scripture where these ideas are supported, but I cannot begin to claim that I am wiser than the many who have tried to understand the Holy Spirit before me. So I find my wisdom resting in faith and research. And you know what? I'm okay with that. I said before that I believe that there are certain topics that are inarguably black and white. An example of something that is black and white to me would be that Jesus is the Savior of the world through His death and resurrection. Then there are other areas of Scripture that are simply not as clear. The rapture and second coming are good examples of topics that are seemingly less straightforward. That doesn't make them any less true or important. It simply means that we are not wise enough (read as "do not know God's intent enough") to definitively say it is this way or that way. I find that I tend to respect leaders more when they are able to admit that they do not have all the answers. Dr. Tim Keller puts it this way: "It is not always easy or necessary to make distinctions between 'natural talents' and 'spiritual gifts,' since ultimately they are all from the Spirit of God." (Keller 2012)

That being said, I do want to provide some semblance of assistance in understanding the spiritual gifts. There are some who separate the nine gifts listed in 1 Corinthians 12 into three different categories—gifts of revelation, gifts of power, and gifts of inspiration. I see it as a helpful categorical organization. The gifts of revelation are given to reveal truth. It can either be a statement of truth that will then be explained or simply a truth revealed to the individual who experiences the gift. The gifts of power serve to show the mighty hand of God in an incredible and clearly supernatural way. The gifts of inspiration serve to encourage and exhort those who hear the message given.

Here is a brief explanation of each of the gifts listed in 1 Corinthians 12:7—10:

1. Wisdom is considered a gift of revelation. It is supernatural guidance or what many understand as prophesying. It's the inexplicable ability to understand the mysteries of the gospel and to then be able to share that understanding with those around them. Simply put, it is the Holy Spirit sharing the mind of God.

2. The gift of knowledge is also a gift of revelation. It is having supernatural knowledge or information that you would not otherwise know. An example of this would be when Jesus knew the history of the woman at the well. It can also be the ability to have a supernatural understanding of a difficult situation and to then be able to give godly advice.
3. The gift of faith is called a gift of power. Even though it is regarded as a gift of power, it is a passive gift because the one who experiences the gift is also the one who experiences the miracle. It is a supernatural belief in God to provide for protection and provision of one's needs. I believe that missionaries who survive through financial support experience this gift in amazing and profound ways.
4. The working of miracles is also considered a gift of power. It is the supernatural display of the power of God in which the laws of nature are altered. The difference between the gift of miracles and the gift of healing is that the working of miracles demonstrates the mighty power of God whereas the gift of healing demonstrates the love, compassion, and mercy of God. When Elijah prayed that it would not rain and it did not, he experienced the working of miracles.
5. The gift of healing would be exactly what it sounds like, a supernatural healing of disease and sickness. This is also called a gift of power. There are numerous examples throughout Scripture of the gift of healing. Jesus healed a multitude while He was on earth, ranging from the lepers to the broken to the woman who had been bleeding for decades.

6. The gift of prophesy is called a gift of inspiration. First Corinthians 14:3 states its purpose is to edify, exhort, and comfort. It does not necessarily relate directly to revelation of information (which would be the gift of knowledge or wisdom). Rather it is an inspired word that will always agree with Scripture. The book of Psalms is a beautiful example. It can be used by the Spirit to explain Scripture.
7. The discerning of spirits is also a gift of revelation. It in itself is an insight into the spirit world. Visions of God would be a manifestation of this gift. It can give insight to the disposition of a person (good or evil tendencies) as well as reveal the presence of a demonic power possessing or oppressing someone. This was especially important in the early church to distinguish between true and false prophets. I believe that this is still incredibly important to covet because of the nature of our society. There are a lot of well-intentioned people who are spewing horrible counterfeit ideas. By the gift of discerning spirits, we can confidently know what is of God and what is false.
8. The gift of tongues is the power to speak supernaturally in a language that is unknown by the people possessing the gift (unless they also are gifted with the final gift, which is the interpretation of tongues). The gift of tongues is meant to catch the attention of others and to indicate the presence of God in a place. Probably one of the most known examples was the day of Pentecost found in Acts. These supposedly simple-minded men began

speaking in languages they didn't know. All of the people around them knew that they had been with Jesus and took notice.

9. The gift of the interpretation of tongues is obviously to interpret the word that was given by the person that had the gift of tongues. This does not refer to people who are naturally gifted in languages. Both the gift of tongues and the interpretation of tongues are gifts of inspiration. As stated before, the difference in spiritual gifts and natural talents is the manifestation of the Spirit. If you can accomplish the task without the help of the Holy Spirit, it's safe to say that it is not an expression of having a gift of the Spirit.

Spiritual gifts span so much further than just what you are good at. For these gifts to be able meet the potential that God intended when He gave them to you, there must be a worship mentality. We all have God-given talents and gifts, but to have a worship mentality, you must step outside of yourself and give God the glory. For example, who do I write for? Am I writing *about* God, or am I writing *for* God? Most of the time writing is simply an example of a talent or something that I can utilize as a ministry gift. However, when the Holy Spirit gives me a specific word to share through writing, it can be manifestations of the gift of prophesy. It is about your heart and allowing yourself to listen and obey the Spirit. The gifts of the Spirit are not to advance any particular individual. They are not to be used as a show or to garner attention to the person but rather to be an act in service to God. Francis Chan says this beautifully. "Many have the knowledge but lack the courage to admit the discrepancy between what we know and how we live" (Chan 2009)

Are we allowing our lives to be open to the movement of the Holy Spirit? Or are we living our lives so structured and impenetrable that even the method in which we worship God is dictated by our need for control, thus diminishing the opportunity to see and experience the might and wonder of the Holy Spirit working in and through us?

Chapter 5 Review

Focus points

- We receive the gifts of the Spirit after salvation.
- The spiritual gifts exist to show people the power of God "so the body of Christ might be built up."
- The use of the spiritual gifts is grounded in worship.

Taking a Step over the starting line

- Have you ever experienced one (or more) of the gifts of the Spirit?
- What are some examples for how spiritual gifts can build up the body of Christ (i.e., the church and fellow believers)?

Chapter 6

Faith in the Spirit

How are we *living* in the Spirit? Second Corinthians 4:7–11 reads,

> But we have this treasure in jars of clay to show that this all-surpassing power is from God and not from us. We are hard pressed on every side, but not crushed; perplexed, but not in despair; persecuted, but not abandoned; struck down, but not destroyed. We always carry around in our body the death of Jesus, so that the life of Jesus may also be revealed in our body. For we who are alive are always being given over to death for Jesus' sake, so that his life may be revealed in our mortal body.

Society tells us that we can be anything that we want. Even if you listen to the messages found in classic cartoon movies, we are told that if we try hard enough, put in the hard work, and wish upon a star, we can get anything we dream. It is extremely important to dream and to have goals; they can help keep us moving forward. But the problem is that we treat the Spirit as something that we can throw on when we feel like it and discard when He may conflict with our earthly desires. When we make a commitment to follow Jesus and give our hearts to Him, we can't just take it back to fit our desired lifestyles.

One of my favorite classic Christian authors is A. W. Tozer. I find him to be insightful in such a realistic and down-to-earth manner that I am often humbled by his words. He said, "To expose our heart to truth and consistently refuse or neglect to obey the impulses it arouses is to stymie the motions of life within us and, if persisted, to grieve the Holy Spirit into silence."[3]

Can you even comprehend grieving the Holy Spirit? We use terms like grief in such flippant terminology that lightens the depth of the original language. A prime example of this in this particular instance is a phrase from one of my favorite cartoons, *Peanuts*. We all know Charlie Brown for the awkward kid who can't seem to catch a break and for his infamous usage of the phrase, "Good grief!" I have a hard time containing my laughter whenever I hear that phrase or catch myself saying it because all I hear in response is the quick wit of my husband saying, "Grief is not good." But even as we use this as a joke amongst ourselves, he is in every way correct.

Grieve is from the Latin word *gravare* or the Middle English word *greven*. It literally means to burden, and it is derived

---

[3] While the quote is by A.W. Tozer, I actually read it in Francis Chan's book, *Forgotten God*.

from a word that means heavy. It can explain a mental distress or the action of oppressing.

When we grieve the Holy Spirit, we are oppressing Him with a heavy burden. We can't just choose to like where God is leading us one day and wish that He would just be silent the next. It is through our lives and through the usage of our gifts that God is revealed every day to the people around us. Living by the Spirit must become continuous interaction and communication with Him. It is realizing that being filled with the Spirit did not just occur in Acts but that we are in the midst of an active relationship and pursuit of God. (Chan 2009)

This active pursuit of God is not without risk. We build up our own little comfort zones and close out the rest of the world—both the dangers and the potential for greatness that exist in it. Think of it as our own inflatable bubble specially designed to keep certain parts of the world out. We have our bubble that we walk gingerly within and pray that something doesn't come along and pop it.

We thank God for the blessings He has provided and feel sad when we see a homeless man, disheveled and unbathed, sleeping beneath the freeway. Beside him is a single shopping cart that holds all of his earthly belongings. "Oh," we say to ourselves, "I wish we could do more to help." Then we turn away, blow up our little bubble, and don't dare to step closer to that man at the possibility that our little world could be torn beyond mending.

We like the idea of sending a check, but if we are given an opportunity to go in, get our hands dirty, and experience the real pain and disparity firsthand, our bubble is blown up around us. Because we maintain this comfort zone, we shrink our potential to change the world.

I once heard it said that when we bring God down to our level, we are left with a God that can't astonish us. We like God to fit inside our lives, our bubbles, rather than chasing after Him. God has gifted us all with such unique gifts that when we settle to live within our comfort zones, we are settling to live safe. Mark Batterson says, "Jesus didn't die to keep us safe; he died to make us dangerous." (Batterson 2013)

If each of us took a single step outside of our own little safety bubbles, what would we be able to accomplish? I'm not even suggesting extreme change. I am proposing that we each take a single step outside. That single step would open doors to such a drastic change that we can't even imagine it.

Kenneth E. Hagin said, "When you volunteer to work for God, he is liable to promote you." (Hagin 2011)

God told the people of Israel, "If you are willing and obedient, you will eat the best from the land" (Isaiah 1:19).

How do we step out of our comfort zones to obey the prompting of the Holy Spirit and to allow God to begin a work in each of us? Through one simple word that is never as easy to follow—*faith*.

Just as we briefly discussed right at the beginning, faith in God is paramount to *doing* anything. In order to move forward, we need to believe that we are moving in the right direction, which in the case of this book is the direction that God has called us to move. Ephesians 1:18–20 says,

> I pray that the eyes of your heart may be enlightened in order that you may know the hope to which he has called you, the riches of his glorious inheritance in his holy people, and his incomparably great power for us who believe. That power is the same as the mighty strength he exerted when he raised Christ from the dead and seated him at his right hand in the heavenly realms.

The word *believe* in the New Testament is typically translated from the Greek word *pistis*, which means "assurance belief, believe, faith, fidelity." In most instances, the word faith is translated from this same word and thus can be used interchangeably more often than not. (Moore 2004) So when I say that I have faith in God, it can equally be said that I believe God. The difference in my mind when I read those two related phrases is that one stands out as a submissive phrase and the other is action-oriented. When I have faith in God, it's almost as if I can cheer Him on from the sidelines, never changing my involvement. When I believe God, I feel as though I need to do something about it. That is my source of inspiration.

The reality is that our goal, the pinnacle for our lives, is to please God. And Scripture tells us that our faith is what brings God pleasure. Hebrews 11:6 says, "And without faith it is impossible to please God, because anyone who comes to him must believe that he exists and that he rewards those who earnestly seek him."

Chapter 6 Review

Focus points

- We are called to continually live by the Spirit.
- When we ignore the prompting of God, we grieve the Spirit.
- Living by the Spirit involves continuous interaction and communication with Him.
- Our comfort zones prevent us from fully realizing God-given opportunities.
- God will equip us if we are simply obedient in faith.
- Believing in God and having faith cannot be separated.

Taking a Step over the starting line

- Where are places in your life where you can step out of you bubble to be obedient to the prompting of the Spirit?
- Why do you think you retreat to your comfort zone in the first place?

Chapter 7

Reflections Stand Out from the Crowd

The Bible tells us that at the end of time all will bow before the Lord, honoring and worshipping Him. We correspondingly seek to please God because it is only through Him that we exist at all. Revelation 4:11 reminds us of this when it says, "You are worthy, our Lord and God, to receive glory and honor and power, for you created all things, and by your will they were created and have their being."

Within our gifts we are never called to be comfortable. God gives us gifts that will stretch us, pull us, and twist us in ways that we would never attempt or even desire on our own. That's kind of the point. Why give us something that we can fully use to its full capacity on our own strengths and abilities? The point of giving us the gift in the first place is not just to bless our lives with unique individuality and personality but to draw us closer to God as well. Everything in life comes back to that very idea. We are created for a purpose, and that purpose is to worship God fully with everything we've got. We are to use every gift and ability to reach out to the heavens and be a light on the hill. We are to be that light pointing others back to

God. It is the relationship with us that brings God pleasure and glory.

If we continue to simply mull around in those areas that we are most comfortable, why would we bother asking God to help? Have you ever noticed that your closest friends are the ones who have gone through the most with you? They are the ones who have been there through thick and thin and never left your side. They are the ones who have seen you at your worst and still choose to love you. In those times when you have fallen, they are the ones who are there to help you back to your feet and wipe you off. That is who God desires to be in our lives. His gifts and commands aren't just there to fill pages of a good book. They are to guide us when we fall. They are to give us encouragement when we are at our weakest and to pull us back to our feet when we have fallen on our faces. His gifts to us are to deepen our need for Him and thus strengthen our relationship because of the pure necessity to trust Him. And because of that trust, He has called us to be obedient with those gifts.

What was the final command Jesus left His disciples with before He returned to heaven? "Therefore go and make disciples of all nations, baptizing them in the name of the Father and of the Son and of the Holy Spirit, and teaching them to obey everything I have commanded you" (Matthew 28:19–20).

Jesus' last command can be simplified into a single word—*go*. It's a command, not a suggestion. It is a simple directive that leaves no room for question, complaint, or confusion. And yet we (more often than not) respond with a resounding no.

Who are we to do anything except obey? And still we are audacious enough to cast this instruction aside as though it were merely another man's suggestion.

The challenges that come with living a life that is fully devoted to finding purpose and fulfillment could fill a library of books. As Christians, we are held to a higher standard by those who know us and respect us. We are also held to a different standard by those who despise and wish only that we fail miserably. Ultimately we are held to a higher and better standard by Jesus Himself. We are told to live *in* the world and not *of* it.

Great, another one of those churchy phrases that we all say but don't really know what it means or what it looks like in real life outside of Jesus telling an interesting story. This one in particular raises quite a quandary among a lot of people.

How can I live in the world but not of it? How do you live *of* something in the first place?

I think about my home. I live in my home. Okay, got that part. Now how am I a part of that home? I am not a part of the walls or foundation, but if I weren't there, would it be the same?

When I look at the world that we live in, I am overwhelmed by the attacks that come my way the second I say openly that I am a Christian. Some are other Christians who are looking to judge just how good of a Christian I am by their own standards. Others are not believers but individuals who are looking to judge just how much of a failure I am and how they can turn that against the validity of my beliefs. This is it. I live here. Like it or not.

The challenge is to refrain from being *of* the world. Think of it this way: Don't lower your standards out of convenience and instead live by God's standards. We can't change what Scripture says just because it's difficult to understand or because other people don't want to follow it. God's Word tells us that nothing should be added to or taken from the Word of God. It is written. It is finished. I may not like everything that is written, but that is the guideline that I choose to live my life by.

Choosing to live that life, one without compromise, is how we refrain from being *of* the world. When people see you on the street, do you blend in or stand out? The actions you take or the words you say can cause you to stick out from others around you. But more than anything, the reactions you have when things don't go according to plan can show you and those around you where your heart is focused.

When someone cuts you off in traffic, do you curse at them, even if it is under your breath or only in your head? Do you smile at strangers, especially the ones who almost seem to growl when they walk by? Do you say thank you and mean it?

Those aren't life-changing examples, but speaking from experience, when I was working in sales, I relished the pleasant customers. My entire day could be improved by a genuine thank-you or even a true smile when the person said hello. So many people in this world walk around mad or have a chip on their shoulder, blaming everyone else for their bad moods. We shouldn't add to that crowd.

Be *in* the world, not *of* it.

What about those bigger issues? Are we willing to take a stand to speak out for the things that we believe? I am naturally an outspoken person who rarely keeps her opinions to herself. (It has gotten me in plenty of trouble, I assure you.). But when I began to learn when and how to speak out, I knew that I could make an impact. You are just one person, but to quote a great philosopher, "A single grain of rice can tip the scale. One man may be the difference between victory and defeat." (If you knew that was a Disney quote from *Mulan*, you just earned bonus points.) (Cook and Bancroft 1998) We don't know the depth of impact that our lives can make on someone. We cannot assume that our words and actions are so inconsequential as to live a life of oblivion. We affect the world around us. We are supposed to affect the world around us. We are called to be like "a city on a hill that can't be hidden" (Matthew 5:14–16) We are given gifts and talents so that we are equipped to share the love of Jesus wherever we are living. We are not supposed to blend in. We were made to stand out. But it's learning to stand out in such a way that the focus is not on us or our accomplishments. It's learning to redirect that attention to where it really belongs. It allows the focus to return back to the giver of our gift, recognizing that it came from Him and that He deserves the glory. But the wonder and mystery of being obedient and focusing our gifts on God is that in those moments we often find the greatest satisfaction. In honoring God, He in turn blesses us.

So what are your strengths? What do you love to do? Do you find yourself comfortable talking in front of a group or leading a Bible study? Perhaps you are gifted in teaching or in leadership (both ministry gifts). Are you relational and find yourself giving advice? Perhaps you have experienced the gift of exhortation or of shepherding (pastoring). But remember that the gifts of the Spirit are not limited to simply what you like to do and where you are most comfortable. There will be times when they will force you to step so far out of your comfort zone, you know without a shadow of a doubt that the only way they could come to fruition is through the working of God. And that is the point.

Whatever your gifts are, embrace them. Find opportunities to serve with those gifts. If you have the gift of administration, volunteer to help out around the church office. If you have the gift of teaching, sign up to teach one of the Sunday school classes. If you have the gift of music, get on the worship team. Whatever it is, there are places to plug in. Your job is to find them! Then once you are serving in your gift, allow God to grow and stretch you in that role. It won't always be fun, and it may hurt a little; however, the outcome is like that of refined silver. And then as you continue to utilize the gifts God has given you, He will continue to grant you more opportunities to see the Holy Spirit working in and through you.

> Come and see what God has done, how awesome his works in man's behalf! He turned the sea into dry land, they passed through the waters on foot—come, let us rejoice in him. He rules forever by his power, his eyes watch the nations—let not the rebellious rise up against him. "Selah" Praise our God, O peoples, let the sound of his praise be heard; he has preserved our lives and kept our feet from slipping. For you, O God tested us; you refined us like silver. You brought us into prison and laid burdens on our backs. You let men ride over our heads; we went through fire and water, but you brought us to a place of abundance. I will come to your temple with burnt offerings and fulfill my vows to you—vows my lips promised and my mouth spoke when I was in trouble. (Psalm 66:5–14)

When the ironsmith is working silver, he must put it in the coals where it is so hot that it changes the properties of the silver. It is said that he will know when it is ready because he will be able to see his reflection in it. Makes for a perfect illustration, doesn't it? As God works in us and through us, we will find that we are facing trials and tribulations, but David reminds us in this psalm that even when we are laden with heavy burdens, we are still to come to God with praise, for "he who began a good work in you will carry it on to completion until the day of Christ Jesus" (Philippians 1:6). And as we continue to trust God through those challenges, we will find that we reflect the Father just a little more and that we are more prepared to receive the incredible gifts the Holy Spirit has to share with each of us.

Chapter 7 Review

Focus points

- We must rely on God to fully utilize our gifts.
- Our gifts are there to encourage not only others but ourselves.
- We are commanded to go out into the world and use those gifts for God.
- If we are obedient in using our gifts for God, we will stand out from the rest of the world (living a life without compromise).

Taking a step over the starting line

- What areas of your life do you find the most difficult to set yourself apart from the rest of the world?
- Why?
- What are three changes that you can make to live a life without compromise? Write them down and find a friend to help hold you accountable.

Part 2

God's Will, Not Mine

Chapter 8

Running with Direction

When I was in college, I found myself buried in a prejudicial relationship. My parents and many of my friends tried to help me, all strongly advising me to get out of it, but I thought I had something to prove. I wanted to prove that they were wrong, even at the risk of compromising and ultimately to the detriment of myself and my morals. When the rug was pulled out from under me, leaving me bruised and broken, I tried to convolute Scripture to show God that what I wanted should be given back to me. I used verses like Psalm 37:4, which says, "Take delight in the Lord, and He will grant you the desires of your heart." As I prayed, I twisted the words to say that this relationship, this guy, was my desire and that since I was serving God, He should give him back to me.

Seriously what was I thinking? It's rather embarrassing, but I now realize all I was thinking about was my own will and selfish wants. I was thinking that I knew what was best rather than submitting those things (and people) I cared for to God and letting Him decide what was best for me. Thankfully God's will rescued me from that relationship despite my objections, and He put me on a path that led me back to Him as my focal point.

This has always been a difficult point for me personally. As soon as I feel that I have mastered the concept, I find myself in another situation that requires me to let go and let God. The first message that I ever gave was on that very idea. As a senior in high school, I wanted the opportunity to speak at my youth group. I approached the youth pastor, and he agreed. I felt confident in my message predominantly because it was something that I was dealing with at that time. I tried to use little quips to keep the interest of my fellow students, utilized a video clip from Disney and Pixar's *Finding Nemo* to make my point in a creative fashion, and even planned a serious activity to put my message into action. It was a topic that even at eighteen I knew, and yet even ten years later I find it is still one of the lessons that I have yet to master and have to continually submit back to God.

Imagine an arrow. On its own it is nothing more than a stick with a point attached to one end and some feathers attached to the other. By its own powers it can do nothing. It will just lie there with seemingly no direction or purpose. Now introduce the bow. To be created, the bow had to go through great stresses to ensure its success. If too flexible, it will not hold the string taut enough. If it is not flexible enough, it will snap when it's bent so that we can tie the string. The string itself must be strong enough to not only be tied taut but to support the additional stress that pulling the arrow back will create.

Then the two objects are introduced to each other. The arrow is placed on that string and pulled back. The bow will either hold, allowing its string to be stressed, or its string will snap. To get a little nerdy and slightly scientific, the arrow is unleashing the potential energy of the bowstring. Once released, it converts that potential energy into kinetic energy, transferring from the bowstring onto the arrow itself. Quite simply, once that tension is released, it allows the arrow to fly with great purpose and direction. "Show me the right path, O Lord; point out the road for me to follow. Lead me by your truth and teach me, for you are the God who saves me. All day long I put my hope in you" (Psalm 25:4–5).

In the fall of 2013, I shot an arrow for the first time. With my heritage as a country girl and a brother-in-law who collects different weapons, I realize the slight juxtaposition that this creates in my true country claim. But I promise you that it's valid. I'm just slightly more Southern hospitality country rather than someone who went shooting every day after school. That being established and much to my dismay, I'm kind of a poor shot. I was shooting at a practice animal (one that was not alive and had been created specifically for practice shooting), and I hit it once out of the five attempts. I then attempted to shoot some clay pigeons. For those who don't understand what I am referring to, clay pigeons are objects that are propelled up into the air so that people can practice shooting moving targets. It trains you as if you were going to shoot at a duck while it was flying through the air. Knowing my success with the nonmoving object, I wasn't anticipating any great success with something a fraction of the size and flying through the air. I was correct in my assumption. However, my city-boy husband had great success in both.

You see, I had the great intention of shooting with purpose and direction. I released the tension in the bowstring, and it would fly. The arrow would fly in the general direction that I was intending but not with enough capability to allow it to hit the target for which I was aiming.

Thankfully God has a 100 percent success rate hitting the target He is aiming for. His hand is steady, and He knows the tension that we can each sustain before we reach that pinnacle breaking point. He also understands that to shoot the arrow farther, the string must be pulled back farther. If we want to go nowhere and simply fall where we were placed, then the string needs no tension. It simply has to drop to the ground. But to fly—I mean truly fly—a substantial amount of tension must be created.

There is a saying that piddles around Christian circles. "God won't give you more than you can handle." I actually used this in something that I wrote, believing it wholeheartedly at the time. Then I was called out for its fallacy—not by another believer but by one of my husband's closest friends who is a proud atheist and challenger of all things Bible related. While I don't often engage in his challenges, this particular one struck a chord. He actually stated the truth in that what I said was false. If I was only given trials and tests that I could handle, why would I need God?

I *love* that I serve a God that I cannot understand. I love that in the depths of who He is, we find truth and love and mercy and mystery. I know for a lot of people it is that mystery that keeps them from taking the chance in actually getting to know God, and to be honest, there are a lot of times that it completely infuriates me. I have this need for control, and that is something that I know without a shadow of a doubt I will never in my wildest dreams ever come close to grasping. Even after I die and I am in heaven with Him, I believe that there will still be a great mystery to God. However, at that point I won't struggle with my need for control because I will finally be completely, absolutely, 100 percent at peace with that truth.

I don't understand how God knows what I can handle and what I can't. God allows these trials in our lives and already knows if it will be something that is too great by our own power and abilities. He already knows if that trial will in fact pull us in closer to Him and into His arms with grave assurance that He will handle it for us. He also knows if it will push us further away.

God's will is such an ambiguous term that I sometimes find myself overwhelmed by it. Eloquent prayers often include "and let Your will be done" or "if it is Your will." We say it, but do we understand it? After all, we also have free will in the mix. So if there is free will, how can we have God's will?

You see, as believers we have to live in a certain amount of tension. The Bible tells us that we have free will. The Bible also tells us that we serve a God who is omnipotent. He already knows what will happen. Mark 4 tells us a parable about the farmer sowing his seed. As he sows the seed, it lands on different types of soils. Depending on the soil, the seed can either take root, or it will be taken away. Jesus later revealed to the people who asked for further explanation that the farmer is God, the seed is the Word of God, and the soils are the hearts of men. As we read the parable, it is easy to skip over some of the dialogue that is exchanged by Jesus and his disciples.

> When he was alone, the Twelve and the others around him asked him about the parables. He told them, "The secret of the kingdom of God has been given to you. But to those on the outside everything is said in parables so that, 'they may be ever seeing but never perceiving, and ever hearing but never understanding; otherwise they might turn and be forgiven.'" (Mark 4:10–12)

The crowd He was teaching was so large that Jesus had to get in a boat in order to speak to them and not be trampled. There were a few of His closest followers, including the twelve disciples, in the boat with Him. The exchange quoted is not something said to the masses but rather those close to Him who asked for clarification.

Jesus utilized a quote from Isaiah to emphasize His point. The truth and explanation of the parables were not revealed to everyone. It was only revealed to those who leaned in and asked about the mystery. It wasn't obvious to everyone who heard these stories.

For those who have grown up in the church, I believe the explanation of Scripture is something that is taken for granted (I am speaking wholly about myself.) We assume that everyone who hears the stories will understand what they mean. But there we find that tension to which I was referring.

When Jesus quotes Isaiah, it's not an explanation of the story He just told. Rather it's an explanation on how the hearts of men will receive that story. Here He is—God in flesh. He is performing miracles and speaking truth to the masses. And yet He is telling these few that most will not understand. He is explaining that there is no way that we can fully grasp what these parables are telling us without God revealing it to us. This is emphasized later in the chapter. "He did not say anything to them without using a parable. But when he was alone with his own disciples, he explained everything" (Mark 4:34).

By speaking in parables Jesus was able to reveal either belief or unbelief in the hearts of the hearers. For those who heard and wanted to understand more, the mysteries were revealed. For those who heard and didn't understand but also didn't take the time to seek that understanding, their unbelief was confirmed in their hearts. The understanding of that alone can only be held by an omnipotent God. For who else can know the hearts of those who hear His truths?

We are not the judge of who believes and who doesn't. We simply seek the will of God, and in doing so, we must continue to lean in and to understand the truths and great mysteries that surround that very ideal.

Chapter 8 Review

Focus points

- The will of God won't always line up with what we think we want or need.
- Challenges will either bring us closer to God or push us further away. Only He knows which it will be.
- We will understand God's will more as we seek to understand it more.

Taking a step over the starting line

- What challenges have you faced (or are currently facing) that make it difficult to trust that God knows what is best for you?
- Find a verse in the Bible that resonates with you and your challenge. Memorize it and use it as a prayer as you seek to understand God in a new and greater way.

CHAPTER 9

An Eternal Focus

The Lord will fight for you, and you have only to be silent.
—Exodus 14:14

Our God will fight for us.
—Nehemiah 4:20

They will fight against you, but they shall not prevail against you, for I am with you, declares the Lord, to deliver you.
—Jeremiah 1:19

And I will make you to this people a fortified wall of bronze; they will fight against you, but they shall not prevail over you, for I am with you to save you and deliver you, declares the Lord.
—Jeremiah 15:20

The Old Testament tells the history of a chosen people who would love God for a little while but then turn their backs on Him whenever it was inconvenient. This scenario repeats itself over and over again as the people grow in faith and then falter in their obedience and dedication.

They would try their best to follow the commands that God set before them, but then it would become too difficult and challenging than they wanted or anticipated. God set challenges before them, and He knew there was absolutely no way they could overcome them within their own strength. But God could. When they let go of their own pride and turned back to God, admitting their inadequacies, He welcomed them back without question and took care of the problems for them.

God's will always prevail despite our vain attempts to intercept, disrupt, or even improve our situation. Nothing we do will change it.

"In the beginning God created the heavens and the earth... and He saw that it was good" (Genesis 1:1). One of the great mysteries of God is His omniscience. He already knows what will happen, when, and ultimately why. God's will is simply His dreams and desires for us. You see, more than anything else, God wants us to know Him and to be known by Him. But what does this look like?

We already discussed the challenge that lies in living in that tension between free will and God's omniscience. But to actively live in God's will, we must have a unique lifestyle that sets us apart from others. It takes living a holy life. Holy simply means *set apart*, and that is what we are called to be.

It looks like living for the eternal rather than the temporary. What is eternity? In Scripture the word *eternal* is used to describe an immeasurable period of time. Using the Hebrew Old Testament word *'olam* or the Greek New Testament world *aion* or *aionos*, we see that both literally refer to time or unlimited duration. Aristotle used *aion* to explain the principle that sums up all existence. (Orr 1915) In the plainest terms, eternity is beyond time. It is what exists beyond our physical selves and beyond our physical world and what slips into the metaphysical that science fiction uses as its platform for many incomprehensible story lines. Only this isn't science fiction. It is more real than you could ever imagine. It is immeasurable and infinite. It is God.

> It is written: "I believed; therefore I have spoken." With that same spirit of faith we also believe and therefore speak, because we know that the one who raised the Lord Jesus from the dead will also raise us with Jesus and present us with you in his presence. All this is for your benefit, so that the grace that is reaching more and more people may cause thanksgiving to overflow to the glory of God. Therefore we do not lose heart. Though outwardly we are wasting away, yet inwardly we are being renewed day by day. For our light and momentary troubles are achieving for us an eternal glory that far outweighs them all. So we fix our eyes not on what is seen, but on what is unseen. For what is seen is temporary, but what is unseen is eternal. (2 Corinthians 4:13–18)

As followers of Jesus, we have confidence that we will spend eternity in heaven, basking in the glory and magnificence of God. That is the point. That is what this verse from 2 Corinthians is saying. We believe that God raised Jesus from the dead and has likewise taken our sinful lives and raised them out of sin. He redeems us so that we can in turn tell others about this redemption. It is hard. Paul phrases it by saying that "outwardly we are wasting away." Our bodies are temporary. Anyone who has ever sustained an injury or who has had to watch as a loved one suffered from a disease can attest to that. The trials and tribulations that we deal with each and every day are not for nothing. They serve the purpose of "achieving for us an eternal glory that far outweighs them all." And because of that amazing truth, we focus on the eternal. That is why we look toward heaven with great hope and expectation.

This is a challenge to change what has become the *natural* way of doing things. We hear people that say *"Carpe diem,"* which means, "Seize the day." They say, "Live every day like it your last," "Live like you were dying," or more recently, "YOLO," an acronym for "You only live once. If that means telling as many people as possible about the love and grace of Jesus because you may not be here tomorrow, great! If it means throwing caution to the wind and living solely for your own selfish pleasures, you are missing the entire point of why you are living and breathing today.

At the beginning of time humans were created as eternal beings. Death was not a part of God's perfect creation. There was no pain; there was no death. Death is a direct result of sin's infiltration on God's masterpiece. We were created to be eternal, but with broken worlds come broken bodies. And with broken bodies come a broken mind. We get selfish. We want what we want and not what God wants. We want instantaneous and temporary enjoyments. That is why people get drunk "to forget." It is a temporary fix. That is why people give in to sexual temptation. It meets their temporary physical desires. That is why people hurt one another. It fixes their temporary need for vengeance, justice, or redemption. The world looks to put a Band-Aid on an injury that requires massive surgery. God seeks to make us new.

With an eternal focus we are able to see God's will and plan in and for our lives.

Chapter 9 Review

Focus points

- God's will is eternal and will always prevail.
- Living eternally means living a life set apart (holy).
- Eternity equals God, and likewise God equals eternity.
- Our goal should not be to live for the next big thrill (YOLO).

Becca Ramirez

Taking a step over the starting line

We read in 2 Corinthians 4:18 that we should "fix our eyes not on what is seen, but on what is unseen. For what is seen is temporary, but what is unseen is eternal."

- What does this look like in your everyday life?
- How can your lifestyle reflect that you are set apart?

Chapter 10

Working toward a Perfect Reflection

There are times when I look at my life and the blessings in it and honestly think to myself, *I know that it will be pure, unadulterated paradise with Jesus in heaven, but I like my life. I am enjoying the blessings that God has given me through my family, my friends, and my church. I know that it will be better when Jesus comes back for us, but I could wait. At least for right now.*

Then I can almost immediately counter that by the thought, *What am I thinking? Of course I am ready for Jesus to come back. I will be in paradise. I won't be suffering. My family won't ever suffer again. What is there to think about?*

We cannot fully comprehend what it means to look toward paradise, so I have tried to break it down in my own mind in an attempt to grasp even a sliver of what paradise will be. This is what I came up with. I imagine the most beautiful sight I have ever seen. I imagine a glorious sunset bursting in vibrant hues of oranges and reds shifting into royal violets, purples and blues, golden fingers reaching across a lavish, gem-colored blanket and wrapping me in its beauty.

I imagine the happiest moments in my life. I think of the night my husband proposed to me. It was a cool Florida November night. We were on the beach where I grew up. The night was clear, only a few clouds brewing over the ocean in the distance but not so much that you couldn't see the twinkling stars covering the expanse of the sky. I could hear the sound of the waves as they hit the beach. I could even taste the salt in the air as I breathed in the beauty.

I remember the night my daughter was born. I vividly recall the moment I heard her cry as the cool air of the hospital room filled her lungs. I remember looking into her deep brown eyes for the first time, and in that moment I understood what true sacrificial love felt like.

I think of these precious moments and remember that those seemingly perfect moments are broken and bruised by the sin that fills our world. They are not even close to perfect, though they feel perfect. They feel like the most wonderful, pristine, beautiful moments that could ever exist. But they are about as perfect as that moment you take your dog out for a walk in the pouring rain and end up stepping in a giant pile of dog poop. Perhaps that analogy is a little too much, but I honestly don't think so.

We think we know what perfection is. We issue perfect tens or 100 percent grades to justify what we view as perfection. We think that we understand what beauty is. Whether it is young women modeling the newest luxurious line of clothing or finding a way to capture the scenery around us, we feel a need to put beauty on display. The reality is that we cannot grasp the true meaning of perfection. We can't fathom it. And because of that, we can't even understand to the full extent of what beauty and perfection are in Jesus Christ. He is perfection. He is pure, unadulterated beauty. His birth in a dingy, disgusting stall and His execution on a tree by means of what is still considered to be one of the most horrific methods of death in all of human history—both of those are pictures of perfection that are nearly impossible to understand. They are pictures of what was required to bring us, a miserable broken people, into perfection. That is the perfection that is in Christ Jesus, the only Son of the living God of the universe. Our view of perfection is a broken mirror because of one tiny word with insurmountable consequences—sin.

I have this theory about sin. What if all sin can be credited back to just a single sin, the sin of selfishness. Think about the garden of Eden. Eve sinned in taking and eating the apple because she wanted more than anything else to possess the same knowledge and wisdom that her Creator had. She responded in a selfish act to try to ascertain this desire despite the warnings. Likewise, Adam sinned simultaneously by not stopping Eve because he was being selfish in only looking after himself rather than protecting the good of his family.

Greed is selfishness toward wanting what you don't have. Adultery is selfishness toward wanting something that someone else has. Thievery, murder, lying, hatred—they are all rooted in a selfish nature that puts you first. That is why Jesus' birth in the manger is so astonishing. The selfish nature of man would require a king to be given his rightful birthrights. It would require that everyone come and worship and respect the king in a manner in which he deserves. Selfishness would require that the most ornate palace be prepared, that servants be ready and willing to assist in the care of the child. Jesus gave up His rights and was born without the true fanfare He deserved. He was born without an audience into a cold, rudimentary barn. Surrounded only by animals and a few lowly shepherds who were appointed the privilege of seeing the glory of heaven shine down as it brought forth the good news of the birth of the Christ, Jesus was born. It was the greatest miracle in all creation, and no selfishness was present to take away from the perfection of His birth.

The understanding of God's will can be developed by living from the inside out. When my husband and I got married, my cousin played his guitar and sang while we held Communion. Overwhelmed by making so many other wedding decisions, I opted to let him decide what song he wanted to perform, and he selected a song by Hillsong United titled "From the Inside Out." The chorus reads, "My heart and my soul, I give you control. Consume me from the inside out. Lord, let justice and praise become my embrace, to love you from the inside out. Your will above all else, my purpose remains. The art of losing myself in bringing you praise." (Houston 2006)

I remember figuring out at one point in high school that speaking my opinion to my mom was not always wise and would get me in more trouble. I devised a plan that I thought would be foolproof. I just wouldn't speak. Perhaps you remember when you were little and everyone told you, "If you don't have anything nice to say, don't say anything at all." That became my mantra. Just keep my mouth shut. However, one problem surfaced to demolish my ingenious plan. My face spoke louder than any of the words I actually said. No matter how hard I tried, I could not keep the thoughts I was thinking from showing on my face. Even without saying a word, my mom knew exactly what was going through my head, and it did not bode well for my social calendar.

Jesus said it perfectly when He said, "The good man brings good things out of the good stored up in his heart, and the evil man brings evil things out of the evil stored up in his heart. For out of the overflow of his heart his mouth speaks" (Luke 6:45).

We are taught to be nice to one another. We are told from a young age to keep the mean things to ourselves. But Jesus tells us that that isn't enough. We cannot just put on a nice face and bite our tongues. We have to actually "love our enemies and pray for those who persecute" us. Sure, we can bring ourselves to be nice to people we don't like, but can we love them? That is a whole different thing. That is really hard. If we were to examine our hearts, what would we find? If it is ill will and frustration, that is what will come out of our mouths. Instead we have to seek God to give us heart transplants. We have to change our entire way of thinking. We have to look at each person the way that God does, namely with love and mercy.

Why? Because what it all boils down to is that life is not about me! Want to hear something that may floor you? It's not about you either. "For by him all things were created: things in heaven and on earth, visible and invisible, whether thrones or powers or rulers or authorities; all things were created by him and for him. He is before all things, and in him all things hold together"(1 Colossians 1:16–17 ESV).

Without Jesus, there is nothing. Everything is created by Him, for Him, and through Him. Jesus is a part of everything and everybody. When we treat someone badly, we are treating Jesus that way. When we yell at someone, we are yelling at Jesus. When we wish ill will against someone, we are wishing ill will against Jesus. There is *nothing* outside of Jesus.

We were created for a purpose. We were gifted by the Spirit in amazing and unique ways to bring God glory through our lives. For His glory He has allowed us to be redeemed and forgiven through believing in Jesus as Lord and accepting the sacrifice that He made for us on the cross to pay the penalty of our sins. For His glory He has taken us and is molding us like pieces of clay to be made new.

Ephesians 4:22–24 says, "You were taught, with regard to your former way of life, to put off your old self, which is being corrupted by its deceitful desires; to be made new in the attitude of your minds; and to put on the new self, created to be like God in true righteousness and holiness."

Chapter 10 Review

Focus points

- The world's understanding of the word *perfect* is broken.
- Only Jesus equals perfection.
- Selfishness keeps us from truly understanding God's definition of perfection.
- How we act is a direct reflection of our hearts.

Taking a step over the starting line

- Do you really believe that the condition of your heart will directly correlate to your actions?
- If so, what can you do to make the necessary changes to your heart?

CHAPTER 11

Live Like You Believe It

We are only made new through God's grace, and it's because of that grace that we should live lives that shows it. It's not enough to simply believe in God. A quick Google search shows a 2011 Gallup poll stating that when people are asked, "Do you personally believe in God?" 92 percent answered yes.[4] However, when given the opportunity to differentiate between specific beliefs, the number began to quickly drop. It is clear that simply believing in God does very little in terms of eternity.

Think about the story of the Prodigal Son found in Luke 15. This story demonstrates several important points for believers. Firstly we can all relate to the Prodigal Son. He ran away to those desires that he thought were most important. The examples that Jesus gave are just that, examples. He uses the worst, most detestable examples for the Jewish people He was speaking to. When the younger son asks for his inheritance, it was equivalent to telling his father he wished

---

[4] http://www.gallup.com/poll/147887/Americans-Continue-Believe-God.aspx

he was dead. Traveling to a distant land meant somewhere heathen. Even working for the pig farmer combined the travesty of working for a Gentile with working directly with an animal deemed unclean by Jewish culture. The people in the crowd would have known that the son in the story had sinned immeasurably by the time he decided to return to his father's household. But we all can relate to doing something wrong and feeling as though it was too bad to ever be forgiven.

Another point of this story is to let us know that no sin is too small for God to care about. We like to convince ourselves that "this sin isn't that bad," or tell ourselves, "I can take care of this myself." I was amused when I asked a group of sixth through twelfth graders to rank five different sins. The list I gave them included:

- shoplifting
- cheating on a test
- lying to your parents
- speeding
- murder

What I found so amusing was that for each sin, excluding murder, they wanted further explanation and justification. For shoplifting, the rank depended on what was being stolen. (Lip gloss or candy was very low, whereas electronics or jewelry was higher.) Cheating on a test was dependent on if it was a final, a state exam, or a quiz. Lying to parents was determined by what you were lying about. They questioned if speeding was actually a sin or not.

We have been taught to justify our actions, especially the bad ones, by a different standard than what the Bible tells us. Scripture tells us that "all have sinned and fallen short of the glory of God" (Romans 3:23). Period. There are no special circumstances. There are no justifications for what was done or why. We have all fallen. We have all sinned. We are all worthy of living out eternity in hell, forever separated from God. But that's where we can continue to relate to the story of the Prodigal Son. "But while he was still a long way off, his father saw him and was filled with compassion for him; he ran to his son, threw his arms around him and kissed him" (Luke 15:20).

The father did not ask what the son had done. He didn't scold him for making such foolish mistakes. He undignified himself, ran to him like a fool, and threw his arms around him to show his love for him. The father forgave his son because he loved him and desperately wanted a relationship with him, not because the son deserved it but because the father was merciful.

Submitting to the will of God has nothing to do with our desires. It isn't something that proves that we are somehow worthy or that we have done enough to deserve it. It is giving the decision-making process back to God (whose it was in the first place), because we know and trust that He will guide us to the best decision anyway. We can't simply believe in God. We have to choose to live daily for God, starting by submitting our will for His.

This includes one of the toughest areas of life—temptation. We deal with challenges in our personal lives, whether in how we look or how we act. We deal with challenges in our social lives on what is permissible and where that infamous *line* needs to be drawn. We deal with it in our professional lives through the ever-changing balance of work and family or deciphering the difference between obeying the boss and honoring your own morals. Every aspect of our lives is affected by temptation, and that is Satan's goal. He wants us to struggle and suffer. He wants us to say that we can do it on our own and then laugh at our failings. He delights in our mistakes and boasts in our selfish desire to be so incredibly independent that we allow ourselves to become independent from the one who can help us or sometimes carry us through that very struggle.

Temptation is a tricky subject only because we don't like to hear about it. Sure, Jesus was tempted, but He is God after all. But the point is that Satan came and tempted Jesus with those things that he knew Jesus would have wanted the very most at that moment. It's been said that the fruit in the garden of Eden was precisely that one thing that Eve could not resist. The type of fruit was irrelevant. It wasn't the piece of fruit that tempted Eve so much; it was the possibility of knowing more than she did. It was the opportunity to be godlike, and Satan knew that temptation all too well. It was his own downfall. He jumped at the opportunity to make it the downfall of God's great creation, and it was.

Temptation ties back to the idea of our own selfishness standing in the way of trusting God and knowing that he has our best interest at heart. But temptation itself is not the problem; it's giving in to that temptation.

Mathew, Mark, and Luke all tell the story of Jesus' temptation. It begins with a fast. Jesus is seeking God and desiring to be closer to Him prior to beginning His official time of ministry. After forty days He is clearly hungry. Satan tempts Jesus with food, His greatest physical desire at that point. He then tempts His mind, telling Him to prove that He is indeed the Son of God, something that Satan obviously knows, but he also knows that the human heart is weak and prone to pride. Finally his last ditch effort is to tempt Jesus with His position. He tempts Him with that which is already rightfully His as the Son of God. Satan realizes that Jesus wants His kingdom restored and offers it to Him but for a price. (Matthew 4:1–11; Mark 1:12–13; Luke 4:1–13).

Temptation attacks our greatest weaknesses, whether we acknowledge them as the root of the problem or not. Temptation doesn't just fall into a spiritual categorization. It is just as likely to be physical like Satan tempting Jesus to turn a rock into bread. Or it can be mental, forcing us to believe that we are made for so much less and to fall prey to self-doubt and in turn self-abuse. But even within these, temptation is so detrimental because it presents itself as a challenge of our true identity. It becomes a challenge to our faith and who we claim to be in Christ Jesus.

For a long time I dealt with what I thought was just physical temptation. I assumed that was the issue because I always seemed to have to have a boyfriend, and I soon began pushing boundaries that I had previously set. But physical affection was not my actual weakness. I had an irrational fear of being alone.

As I grew older, the only nightmares that I continued to have involved the death of one of my family members as this person saved me from some extravagant scenario (saving me from being eaten by a monster, saving me from a fire, saving me from who knows what but done in an elaborate spy style). The only one who didn't die saving me was the one who died because I couldn't save him. That was the nightmare I had for my husband.

It is clear that my fear was losing the people I knew loved me enough to die for me. My weakness was acknowledging that I couldn't save the person I would willingly die for. My weakness for being alone translated into a variety of sins, but until I understood what weakness Satan was targeting, I didn't know how to combat him. Once I knew, I realized that I could not combat him alone. It had to be God. I had to have the faith to believe God when He told me that even if I lose every person I love, I am still not alone because I have Christ, who lives in me. It came down to a challenge of my identity in Jesus.

There are so many of these temptations that the world tells us are okay. Even in a lot of churches, the Bible is approached as just some out-of-date book that can't deal with the realities of life today. To them, homosexuality, sex before marriage, gambling, and pornography are all just parts of life. All of these come with their own set of challenges and struggles. Pornography is one of those sins that people make excuses for because they claim that it doesn't affect anyone besides themselves. But for those who have been strong enough to admit their sin and seek God and His counsel to battle the temptation, they will be the first to tell you that it will chip away at everything around you and that it is always something that lingers in your mind. The temptation is always there, but through honoring God and seeking His help, they are stronger to fight against it and not as distracted by it.

We all have our forbidden fruit, and no one is strong enough to conquer it in their own strength. Only by submitting to the will of God and allowing Him to be victorious in our lives can we be freed from these ties. We cannot simply adhere to the "we are victorious" mantra, but we must be willing to sacrifice those temptations, those hidden desires to allow Him to be victorious in our lives on a daily (sometimes hourly) basis. We have to allow Him to be the overcomer in our lives. We must acknowledge that we have overcome because God has overcome it *for* us.

Chapter 11 Review

Focus points

- Believing and trusting God goes beyond ritual. It is a way of life.
- Nothing is too small for God to care about.

- Temptation can appear in many forms (physical or mental), but it always attempts to undermine our identity in Christ Jesus.

Taking a step over the starting line

- Is there an area of your life that you have yet to surrender to God?
- What is holding you back from doing so?

Chapter 12

Understanding His Will

Society will tell us that if we live our lives in a manner that is fully dependent on God, we will be zealots. We will be offensive and unloving of those who do not share our same beliefs. The truth is that if we are truly living lives that are sacrificial to God's will, we can't help but love those around us, no matter how they choose to live or what they believe. The true Christian is not offensive. Tozer said, "If we follow Christ, with all the facts before us and knowing what we are about, deliberately choose the Kingdom of God as our sphere of interest I see no reason why anyone should object. If we lose by it, the loss is our own; if we gain, we rob no one by doing so." (Tozer 1948)

Living by the will of God isn't about becoming judge and jury against the rest of the world. On the contrary, it is so far from that point that I think some of the people who claim to be Christian would find themselves left out in the cold. Yes, I am to stand for the Bible and the ways that it instructs me to live; however, I am not the one who decides the heart of those who choose to live otherwise. I am simply called to share what God has told us through His Word and live my life to the best of my ability, honoring that Word but never condemning others by that same Word. That is God's job … and only God's job.

It is a hard line to walk between sharing the truth of God and how He calls us to live and judging someone who does not live that same way. The Bible warns us that we will be judged accordingly. We aren't going to be lined up from most holy to least. We're judged against perfection, and unless we are covered in the blood of Jesus, that judgment will be just the beginning of our eternal hell. There is the proverbial parental example that is used when we get caught and we blame our friends.

"If they were all jumping off a bridge, would you jump?"

Christians do this in our excuses for judging. "Well, Pastor so-and-so said—" Or we say, "My Bible study told me—"

Don't jump. Or in this case, don't judge. We don't know what God is doing in the hearts of those individuals or groups. We don't know what the outcome will be, so don't make the assumption that we somehow do know. Only God knows what lies in the depths of the hearts of man. Only God can see if their heart is malleable for His seed to take root or if it is too hard and has already made the decision to turn away from His love and truth.

That is when we can finally sacrifice our own will to the will of God and step forward in our pursuit of His purpose for our lives.

There are times when I get so encumbered by a phrase that I forget the true meaning of that phrase. "God's will" is one of those. I understand God as Creator, King, and Savior. I know Him as the one who holds my life in His hands. But then we get to the *will*. We have a propensity to understand God's will as a harsh reality that means that no matter what, we have no control over what happens to us or our lives. We see God's will as a violation of our own ideas and desires. We see it as something to resent and balk against. Instead, we miss how beautiful the concept of God's will really is. We miss that it is completely focused on us and what is best for us. We miss that it is the deepest desires of God for our lives. The same way a parent longs for the highest and best for his or her children, so too does God long for the highest and best for His children.

If that is where our heart and focus is, we will miss the beauty that exists through these two simple words. God's will is His desire for us. It is that desire and wish for us carried out.

So what is God's will? According to only a handful of verses, God's will is to be joyful, to pray without ceasing, and to give thanks no matter what the circumstances are (1 Thessalonians 5:18). It is to be sanctified (1 Thessalonians 4:3) and to be filled with the Spirit, worshipping and praising Him with thanksgiving and submitting ourselves to one another so that we do not become selfish or conceited (Ephesians 5:17–21). It is to allow the Spirit of God to transform who we are and change the way we think so that when we need to, we can test and determine for ourselves what is God's will

(Romans 12:2). When we do this, we are promised that He will equip us to do His will (Hebrews 13:21) and that those who do the will of God live forever (1 John 2:17).

In all of these verses the word that is used when one is referring to the will of God is *thelema*.[5] It's a noun that refers to "the purpose of God to bless mankind through Jesus Christ" and what God wishes to be done by us. In short, it is a tremendous blessing to each and every one of us.

What I love is a parallel found in the language used in Psalms. The psalmist says multiple times, "I desire to do your will," or "Teach me to do your will" (Psalm 40:8; 143:10). These particular instances use a Hebrew word *ratsown*.[6] It means pleasure or delight and comes from the root word *ratsah*,[7] which means to be pleased with.

The reality of our seeking God and desiring to do His will is His delight and thus a fulfillment of His will. He is pleased with us when we seek after Him. He finds pleasure in our longing to understand His truths and mysteries. And as we continue to seek to do these things, He will continue to bless us and reveal more of Himself to us.

---

[5] Thayer and Smith. "Greek Lexicon entry for Thelema". "The KJV New Testament Greek Lexicon"

[6] Brown, Driver, Briggs and Gesenius. "Hebrew Lexicon entry for Ratsown". "The KJV Old Testament Hebrew Lexicon"

[7] Brown, Driver, Briggs and Gesenius. "Hebrew Lexicon entry for Ratsah". "The KJV Old Testament Hebrew Lexicon"

Chapter 12 Review

Focus points

- Living a life devoted to God is not offensive; it is loving and generous.
- We are called to love everyone and leave the judgment to God.
- The will of God is a blessing to us.

Taking a step over the starting line

- Do you find it challenging to love others, especially if they have different beliefs than you do?
- In what areas do you find yourself more judgmental toward others? Take time to prayerfully submit those areas to God, asking Him to change your heart so that you can know how to love without condemnation.
- How can we discover God's will for our own lives?

Part 3
Service before Self

CHAPTER 13

Servant Leader

In the church we have a lot of colloquialisms. Servant leader is one of those phrases. We know that being a leader is important, and we understand that we are to serve, so why not sandwich these ideals together to describe the type of leadership that we see in the life of Jesus? The phrase was coined in 1970 by a man named Robert Greenleaf. Greenleaf said, "A new moral principle is emerging, which holds that the only authority deserving one's allegiance is that which is freely and knowingly granted by the led to the leader in response to, and in proportion to, the clearly evident servant stature of the leader." (Greenleaf 1982)

Greenleaf, while he was publishing the official phrase, was not the creator of this ideal. In Mark 10, Jesus taught His disciples this same principle.

> Jesus called them together and said, "You know that those who are regarded as rulers of the Gentiles lord it over them, and their high officials exercise authority over them. Not so with you. Instead, whoever wants to become great among you must be your servant,

and whoever wants to be first must be slave of all. For even the Son of Man did not come to be served, but to serve, and to give his life as a ransom for many." (Mark 10:42–45)

If we want to be successful in achieving all of the greatness that God has planned for us, we must first humble ourselves and serve others.

We all serve something or someone. Some serve money. They are controlled by the need to acquire the newest and greatest. Their lifestyle is never enough, and attaining more simply has to be the answer. Some serve power. Being mediocre is the equivalency to sinning. Their jobs are everything to them, and it takes priority over every other thing in their lives—family, friends, and even morals. They couldn't live with themselves if they were passed up for promotions or they lost their jobs.

Sometimes what we serve doesn't seem bad at the onset. Family, for example, is a wonderful blessing that should certainly be a priority in our lives. But if we serve our families above God, our priorities are still misguided. Sometimes more is not better. It's simply more. More time spent with family doesn't guarantee that time is quality time. Likewise, more activities together don't ensure stronger relationships. How can we possibly hope to understand how to serve and prioritize our families if we don't first learn how to serve and prioritize the God who made us?

I think that Jesus likes to give us paradoxes in our lives. It keeps things interesting, I suppose. The idea of a servant leader is one of those paradoxes. To the world's standards, a leader is not some who is humble and submits to the authority of another. A leader takes charge and accomplishes what needs to be done. The focus of leaders is on their own advancement and success. Jesus took the world's idea and turned it on its head. As a King, Jesus humbled Himself to be no more than any man. He reached out to the ones who had be ostracized from their communities, befriended those who no one wanted as friends, and loved even those who hated Him so much that they crucified Him.

Robert Greenleaf also said, "The great leader is seen first as a servant, and that simple fact is the key to his greatness." (Greenleaf 1982)

To be a good leader, you must first follow. To serve well, you need to understand what it looks like to serve others with a humble heart. Even if you do not have parents who gave up the world to care for you, I am sure that there is someone in your life who has shown you what true service looks like in action.

Maybe it was that teacher who didn't just teach because it was a job but because he or she had a genuine love of teaching and the person truly loved the students. This teacher would put in the extra hours needed if it meant helping just one more child reach his or her full potential. Maybe that teacher was the one soul who didn't just reach your head but reached to your heart. He or she opened your eyes to how incredible learning could be.

Maybe you have friends who have always been there for you. They offer to drive when you don't have a car, or they give you advice in the middle of the night when both of you should be sleeping. Maybe they pray for you when you just don't have the words to explain what is on your heart.

Service can take many shapes and forms, and becoming a servant first will likely prepare you for an opportunity to serve also as a leader. We like to ponder and think about abstract ideas. We pride ourselves on our ability to dissect analytical concepts that we can then criticize for their impunity. But beyond that, how much are we taking the time to think through the more simplistic though immensely more practical question, "What can I do about it?"

This is the area that the world is watching more than any other. Are we who call ourselves Christians only worried about our own well-being? Or are we as Christians taking the example that Jesus led seriously enough to not just read about it but to follow it? We live in a society that looks for ways to tear down someone's belief all while we claim that we desire for everyone to coexist. They would rather everyone believe nothing than believe in Jesus. But what they cannot deny is the effect of a person who serves willing and wholeheartedly. No matter what their personal beliefs, society wakes up and starts paying attention to the actions of individuals who are making a difference in the lives of others.

We need to lead others by first meeting their most rudimentary needs. We need to open our eyes to opportunities to place the well-being of others before ourselves. We need to stop being so focused on the opportunities we are trying to create for others that we miss the opportunities that God has created for all of us to serve one another and thus serve Him. We have so much to offer, and Jesus so often chooses to work through those moments. If we neglect them, we, too, are missing the chance to encounter God on a completely different level than you may have ever experienced.

The Bible tells us that when we serve others, we are in fact serving Jesus.

> For I was hungry and you gave me something to eat, I was thirsty and you gave me something to drink, I was a stranger and you invited me in, I needed clothes and you clothed me, I was sick and you looked after me, I was in prison and you came to visit me. Then the righteous will answer him, "Lord, when did we see you hungry and feed you, or thirsty and give you something to drink? When did we see you a stranger and invite you in, or needing clothes and clothe you? When did we see you sick or in prison and go to visit you?" The King will reply, "I tell you the truth, whatever you did for one of the least of these brothers of mine, you did for me." (Matthew 25:35–40)

In April of 2014, *Relevant Magazine* posted a video of an experiment run by an organization called NYC Rescue Mission. The organization had created a video social experiment showing how invisible we have made homeless men and women. They took family members, dressed them as homeless, and placed them on the street where another family member would walk by. They asked the question, "Have the homeless become so invisible we wouldn't notice our own family living on the street?"[8] The results of the experiment spoke for themselves when none of the individuals noticed their family members sitting on the street. We close ourselves off to things that will make our world *dirty*. I don't mean the literal sense of being dirty, but rather I mean that by allowing ourselves to become interruptible (like Jesus), we would not be able to maintain our strict schedules and expectations.

Have you ever taken the time to look at the circumstances of Jesus' miracles? They weren't planned. He didn't have the disciples round everyone up, stand up on the stage, and select specific people from the crowd who would allow for the ostentatious miracles. He was attending a wedding (John 2:11). He was teaching at the temple (Mark 1:21–28). He was entering the city (Mark 2:1–12). Even when He withdrew from the crowds, they would seek Him out (Matthew 14:13–21). They happened in the moment exactly when they needed to happen.

We, too, need to live lives that are interruptible. We need to serve others, especially when it's not convenient to our set schedules. And when we do stop to serve others, it's not with a begrudging heart. It's with a hopeful attitude,

---

[8] You can check out the video at http://www.makethemvisible.com/

knowing that we are not only serving those individuals but also serving God. We need to take the initiative to help others whenever we can. We don't need to show others how good we are, but we should live lives that show everyone how good our God has made us. It's not a natural reaction, but that is what it means to be a servant leader.

Chapter 13 Review

Focus points

- In order to lead others, we must first serve them.
- Service can take the shape of anything when we are putting others before ourselves.
- Do you need a starting point? Meet someone's physical needs (food, clothing, etc.). Meeting a physical need can open the door to allow God to meet a spiritual need.
- Allow your *plan* to be interruptible.

Taking a step over the starting line

- Name at least one way that you can serve someone this week.
- What keeps you from living an interruptible life?
- How can you change your mentality to better allow for divine interruptions?

Chapter 14

Not a What But a Who

We serve this God, who is so incredible that He wants a people of His own. That's why He created us in the first place. That is also why we as human beings are naturally relational. There are no other religions that have God coming to us. Everything else is about us going to God first. They are focused on doing something. The Pharisees were the same way in Jesus' day. They looked at God as a step-by-step process that originated in their heads as the knowledge of God. It then proceeded to religion as their belief, obedience as the response to their belief, and then finally to discipline as a visible proof of their obedience. They *knew* a lot, so they must have been religious. The idea that they lived by was this: If you are religious, you must be obedient and thus disciplined. Then Jesus came along and turned the whole idea on its head. I love how He does that. Of course, then He does it in my own life, and it's not quite as much fun—perhaps beneficial but not fun. Jesus said the order was (1) love, (2) relational, (3) obedience, and (4) habit. John 14 says, "If you love me, you will obey what I command" (John 14:15). It starts with the heart and having a relationship. From that love and relationship, we long to obey. The more we obey, the more it becomes habitual. The initiation of the entire process is built within the relationship we have with Jesus.

Because of that, our purpose is never just a *what*. It is a *who*. Acts tells the story of Paul and the man God used to change his life.

> And he said, "Who are you, Lord?" And he said, "I am Jesus, whom you are persecuting. But rise and enter the city, and you will be told what you are to do." The men who were traveling with him stood speechless, hearing the voice but seeing no one. Saul rose from the ground, and although his eyes were opened, he saw nothing. So they led him by the hand and brought him into Damascus. And for three days he was without sight, and neither ate nor drank. Now there was a disciple at Damascus named Ananias. The Lord said to him in a vision, "Ananias." And he said, "Here I am, Lord." And the Lord said to him, "Rise and go to the street called Straight, and at the house of Judas look for a man of Tarsus named Saul, for behold, he is praying, and he has seen in a vision a man named Ananias come in and lay his hands on him so that he might regain his sight." But Ananias answered, "Lord, I have heard from many about this man, how much evil he has done to your saints at Jerusalem. And here he has authority from the chief priests to bind all who call on your name." But the Lord said to him, "Go, for he is a chosen instrument of mine to carry my name

before the Gentiles and kings and the children of Israel. For I will show him how much he must suffer for the sake of my name." So Ananias departed and entered the house. (Acts 5:5–17)

God's placement of Ananias in Paul's life allowed him to be a catalyst for telling the world about Jesus. In many of our lives we are able to define that one person who has made a tremendous difference in our lives and given us the needed direction. For me, it is my mom. Of course, all moms have this distinct way of influencing our lives in ways that we may or may not want, but my mom has done more than just teach me right from wrong. She has been the fuel to my passions.

Kay Shinn was raised in a home that was not filled with warm, fuzzy feelings of love and encouragement. Dealing with adversity from her family and many of the others who crossed her path shaped her to be strong-willed and strong-spirited. Little did she know that this would become a hereditary trait passed on to her youngest daughter.

I was born stubborn. Even my pediatrician told my mom, "She's a leader, Mommy Shinn, not a follower." (I was still only a toddler at the time.) But as I grew I began to use this leadership strong-willed quality against my mom. By the time I was in high school, we would not just argue. We would yell. It is one of those memories lodged in my brain that I look back on and cringe, simultaneously praying that my daughters will somehow skip over the teen years and that I will be saved from the payback that is most likely coming to me. I was wrong in so many ways, but through all of it, my mom loved me. She encouraged my strong-willed nature. When people didn't understand me, she would comfort me and hold me tight, telling me that it was okay. She was my rock when everything I thought was true began to crumble. The reason that she was able to be that for me was because she was simultaneously directing my focus back to Jesus.

Craig Groeschel says it in a fantastic way that made me think of my mom's (and dad's) leadership in how I was raised. "What is priority one? I believe our greatest priority as Christian parents is to gradually transfer our children's dependence away from us until it rests solely on God." (Groeschel 2011)

Parents have this incredible responsibility to help "train up a child in the way he should go" (Proverbs 22:6), and their impact is something that oftentimes gives either endless possibilities or continual challenges to overcome. It's easy to recognize the impact (good or bad) that parents will have on their children, but it is just as vital that we look at the impact we can have on our friends, classmates, coworkers, or even strangers. We cross paths with people, whether we want to or not, and we can make an impact even in a single line of conversation.

Let's use the example of a grocery store cashier. She has been there since the crack of dawn, standing on her feet the entire time without a break and dealing with a hoard of customers who are arguing over the store's coupon policy, the limited selection of Asian specialty foods, even the pricing on food (because she has so much control over that). Needless to say, it has been a difficult morning, and she is working a double shift today to try to make ends meet. Then you come along. Maybe you are having a difficult day too, but what if you focus on sharing the love of Christ instead of grumbling about the wait time to check out?

When I worked in sales, those customers who were cheerful and encouraging could change my outlook completely. Even a simple but genuine thank-you made a world of difference when the rest of the day had been filled to the brim with grumblers.

Our purpose is not accomplished by putting on the blinders and trying to hammer the gospel down one person's throat. Even if we do manage to share with the right person, what about the thousands of other people we will encounter throughout our life spans?

Matthew 5:7 says, "God blesses those who are merciful, for they will be shown mercy." When we begin to live lives that look to others before they look to our own selfish desires, we begin to understand compassion in the way that Jesus meant it. To know Jesus is to ultimately know mercy.

How can mercy direct our lives? If we begin to understand that our purpose is never for ourselves but for others and in bringing God glory, we begin to get past one of our biggest obstacles—ourselves and our own desires.

Jesus told us that we are to be "the salt of the earth" (Matthew 5:13). Why? The entire purpose for salt is to make something better than it is on its own, enhancing or preserving the flavor of the food. In the days of the Roman Empire, salt was of equal value to oil today. Soldiers were even paid in salt. It was a precious and valuable commodity. (Cowen 1999) But if salt lost its saltiness, it was beyond worthless. It no longer made things better. It made them worse.

If we are to live the way that the gospel tells us, we must look beyond ourselves. We have to live out what we believe and not just know the information. What good is it to be able to quote the Holy Scripture if our lives do not reflect the truths we are speaking? The same Spirit that raised Jesus from the dead is the same Spirit that resides in all those who believe the gospel.

I have no doubt that God knows the name of someone we will directly impact, but who is to say that we will only affect one person? The average American has a life expectancy of just less than eighty years. That is a long time to encounter a lot of people. Different times in our lives will allow for different opportunities. What stage of life we are in can minister greatly to someone in that same stage. Or perhaps someone has already gone through a similar experience as another person. One does not have to be in the midst of a situation to be able to relate to the challenges and to share God's love.

When I was in the midst of the challenges I faced in college, I was not equipped to be an effective leader to students.

However, several years removed, I was able to offer an understanding ear to some of the high school students in my church's youth group who were facing similar challenges to the ones that God had seen me through. The first time I shared my story I was scared. I was scared about the possible judgment from both the students and their parents. I was scared about not meeting the expectations of those I was serving alongside. I was scared that somehow I wasn't good enough to be utilized in the lives of these students. But God can use any moment in a person's life to bring Him glory so long as we are obedient to serve Him with that life.

Ananias was scared but he followed God's call. Because he was obedient, the gospel began to reach the corners of the earth and into the hearts of every man.

Chapter 14 Review

Focus points

- To serve God, you must first have a relationship with Him.
- Obedience is a response to that relationship.
- Serving God is not always about *what* we are doing but *who* we are doing it with.
- Serve others with great mercy.

Taking a step over the starting line

- Is your faith built in a relationship with Jesus or in religion?
- Is there someone in your life who would benefit from having a relationship with Jesus?

CHAPTER 15

Serving in the Day to Day

Service, as an economic term, is an intangible equivalent of an economic good. Remember hearing about the barter system in history class? It serves the purpose of meeting a desire or need. But speaking clinically doesn't come close to providing true understanding of what service means for God.

Vista Community Church in Orlando, Florida, has been putting special focus on serving the community for a number of years. Their mission statement is "connecting people with God," and they actively pursue that statement through reaching out to everyone around them. When someone says, "Mission trip," a trip to your backyard is usually not the first thought to cross your mind. But they have taken an old idea and revamped it. They challenge church members to be missionaries in their neighborhoods, in their schools, and in their offices.

They have even created an event called Vista Serves. The entire church is invited to come and split up into different groups, and then they simply go out and do whatever needs to be done. That could mean helping a church family with a building project when they don't have the money to hire the man power needed. It could mean helping an elderly widow with her much-needed yard work. It may mean helping watch some of the children of other adults in the church so they are able to serve as well.

Wherever we are in that moment, we need to look for opportunities to share the gospel.

Jesus said, "But you will receive power when the Holy Spirit has come upon you, and you will be my witnesses in Jerusalem and in all Judea and Samaria, and to the end of the earth" (Acts 1:8).

It is important to notice the order Jesus used. This is the last thing He is saying to them before He leaves earth, so it is safe to say that it is incredibly important. Firstly He tells them that they will receive power when the Holy Spirit has come upon them. We already touched on the Holy Spirit earlier. When the Holy Spirit comes upon you, you begin to reflect the characteristics of the Spirit. You begin to demonstrate what the Bible calls the fruits of the Spirit—love, joy, peace, forbearance, kindness, goodness, faithfulness, gentleness, and self-control. (Galatians 5:22-23)

Next Jesus tells them that they will be His witnesses in Jerusalem, Judea, Samaria, and all the way to the ends of the earth. He starts from their backyards, takes them into their own nations, leads them into nations that are taboo and then beyond their comfort zones in reaching not only the Jews but also the Gentiles who lived throughout the entire earth.

When we look at service, there is a stigma on certain acts. It's nice to serve soup to the homeless in your own town, but it doesn't meet the same standards as the person who travels to desolate West Africa to start an orphanage for children in war-torn areas. But that isn't how Jesus views it. In fact, He said in Matthew 25:40, "Truly, I say to you, as you did it to one of the least of these my brothers, you did it to me."

If people are able to help their neighbors carry in their groceries, they are able to serve Jesus. If people can read to young children at the local library, they are able to serve Jesus. If people are able to serve that bowl of soup at the local homeless shelter, they are able to serve Jesus.

He never said that we had to travel overseas in order to serve Him. There will be those who are called overseas or into extraordinary circumstances, but just because you don't feel God calling you to the mission field, that does not mean that you don't have your own mission field that God has created just so you can serve Him. And it just might be in your backyard. How can you leverage the power given by God to best serve those who are in need?

In another instance of looking up a words in the dictionary, God revealed truth to me in the straightforward definition to a word I have known the meaning of for many, many years. That word is *service*, and it means, "(noun) the act of helpful activity; help; aid. (verb) to make fit for use; to supply with aid or information."

As a believer, I was struck by the relative variation between the definition of service as a noun and service as a verb. In this world, if we claim to be followers of Jesus, we are service. We are the aid and help reaching out to those around us. God then services us. When we are born, we are born into a broken and bruised world. We are fit for nothing more than death. The second we begin breathing, a countdown clock until we die also begins. Sorry to be somewhat morbid. However, when we are born again as new believers in Jesus, God services our lives. He makes us fit for use and supplies us with aid and information to better serve those around us.

I said it before, and I'll say it again—there is absolutely, positively no reason why everyone cannot serve. Wherever we are in location, whatever our life situations, we are able to serve God and those around us.

No service is too small if you are doing it in the mind-set of serving not just that person but God as well. Paul says it this way: "Whatever you do, work at it with all your heart, as working for the Lord, not for men" (Colossians 3:23).

We may be ridiculed. You may find yourself having to purposely change your attitude when you are speaking with someone. (I just cringed a little as I wrote that.) We may have to adjust our priorities to put others before ourselves.

The likelihood is that it will be a challenge. It means refocusing our lifestyles to reflect hearts that are set on serving God above all else, no matter the cost.

I get it. We all like simple, easy answers. We like our "get out of jail free" cards and love the idea of serving the God that saved us from certain and most disastrous destruction in our lives and eternity. We like how we feel when we get the opportunity to help make someone's day a little better. But to focus our lives around learning to become a servant is not simple. In fact, it is painfully and embarrassingly difficult. I know that just when I think I'm getting the idea, I realize that I don't have a clue.

Jesus took the form of a servant. He washed the nasty, dirty feet of His disciples to show that He was not placing Himself as any greater than those He walked with on a daily basis despite the fact that He was Lord of the universe and all of creation. He died the death of a murderer. How can we then place ourselves above anyone when Christ didn't even take that position?

If you find that you are still caught up on the last section (spiritual gifts) and want to try to figure out what you are gifted in before you begin serving, just stop right now. Don't think about it, just serve. Find a place that is in need, whether in your church or in your community, and start serving in that position. Either you will be a wonderful addition to their team, or you'll realize that maybe you should be serving somewhere else. That's okay! In fact, it's great. You took a chance and trusted God to use you, and you were obedient. That is what God wants above all else. He wants you to see a need, not question Him whether or not you are qualified, but with a servant's heart, you can go and do what you can to meet that need. God wants us to have enough faith that we are willing to take a few risks. He wants us to trust His sovereignty enough that we are willing to put ourselves out there, where we may be horribly uncomfortable, and we can also know that He loves our obedient hearts and will honor that accordingly.

Service is not about what we want or what we think we need. It's not even about what we may or may not be qualified to do. It is about trusting God to equip us for the tasks that He calls us to, no matter what they look like. It's about knowing that we aren't going to be good at everything but that God will always utilize willing hearts. And that will bring Him incredible glory.

Chapter 15 Review

Focus points

- Service starts in your backyard.
- The emphasis in serving shouldn't be on what you are doing but rather the heart with which you are doing it.
- God services (verb) us so that we can be a service (noun) to others.

- Service is based in trusting God to equip us so that we can honor Him however He has asked us to do so.

Taking a step over the starting line

- What are the reasons you give for why you can't serve?
- How has the fact that God has equipped us to serve changed your perspective on service as a whole?

PART 4

On Your Mark ... Get Set ... Go!

Chapter 16

Well-Laid Plans to Rot

A typical senior year of high school is a compilation of different anticipations—anticipation of sports senior nights, senior proms, of senior skip day, graduation, and college acceptance letters.

It's not uncommon to see seniors getting together with friends and talking about all of their hopes and dreams, many of which are centered on getting into the all-important school of choice. Receiving that acceptance letter validates their belief that they will actually be able to turn their grand ideas into achievable realities. My dream school was the only school I applied to. In previous years I had tossed around a number of different school choices, but when it actually came time to submit the application and wait for the impending decision of acceptance or denial, there was only one for me—the University of Florida.

I was born bleeding orange and blue. It was a family tradition dating back to my grandfather, and it never occurred to me that I would not be accepted. When that envelope came, there wasn't a letter of congratulations to be framed for memory.

Instead I received the apology letter. "We are sorry, but—" It didn't matter what else was written or how carefully the word choice had been selected. I got the rejection letter not once but three times. After the first letter I appealed. Then I got the second letter, and I appealed. The reality that I had to face was that they were not going to accept me into the University of Florida at that time.

I struggled with this for several months and subsequently allowed my life to start spiraling downward. Despite my nosedive, God captured my heart again, and I found the faith that I was missing. I began to trust God again and knew that His plans were better than my own, and I knew that I'd better get back on his path if I wanted to get anywhere in life.

We all have a point where we need to stop sitting and get up and go. We get so caught up in this idea of "what is God's plan for me" that we find ourselves in a stalled position. We are unable to pull from past experiences, and we are unable to propel ourselves into the future of that plan with faith that God will give us direction when we need it.

Jeremiah 29:11 is commonly shared with graduates in one form or another, whether at a senior banquet or through a graduation card. That's not a knock against it. I think that verse holds great encouragement for future success. "'For I know the plans I have for you,' declares the Lord, 'plans to prosper you, not to harm you, plans to give you a hope and a future'" (Jeremiah 29:11). Of course, it is probably a good idea to keep in mind the context of this proclamation.

God spoke this word through His prophet, Jeremiah. At the time the Israelites were captives of Babylon. This is God's assurance to them that He would rescue them from captivity and restore them back to the Promised Land.

Now as much as I found high school to be a prime example of captivity within civilized America, it could not come close to comparing to the circumstances the Israelites were facing in sixth-century Babylon. I'm not saying that this beloved verse is inappropriate to share with our students as they face the great and vast unknown before them. I'm simply saying that what is meant to encourage can indirectly put a tremendous amount of pressure on those with whom it is shared.

For those who have a Christian background, these simple words can represent the epitome of both that which we long for and fear equally. It is a great comfort to know that ultimately God has a plan for our lives. It is a daunting realization that God already has a plan for our lives and that we do not have a clue what it might entail. Even for those lucky individuals who know exactly what they plan to do with their careers, the idea that this plan is all-encompassing can belittle the best laid plans of an individual.

Ultimately whether we feel daunted by the task or maybe that we have already strayed so far from what God must have planned that it feels as though it is hopeless, we are left with the responsibility to get up and follow God to the best of our ability.

The heroes from the Old Testament are sometimes thought to have been these perfect guys who just seemed to get it. They could trust and follow God beyond what we are capable of today. However, that is complete nonsense. So let's revisit Abraham, who was the father to the nations. He is the point of lineage for three of the world's major religions, which is saying quite a lot for a world that is divided by what we believe. But I think one of the best parts about Abraham is that when God came to him with the plan for his life, Abraham was a nobody. He didn't attend the right church or hang out with the perfect Christian crowd. Abraham had married a girl who couldn't bear children and was living in the land of Ur among a tribe of idolaters. And yet when God appeared to him and told him to go, he obeyed.

> The LORD had said to Abram, "Leave your country, your people and your father's household and go to the land I will show you. I will make you into a great nation and I will bless you; I will make your name great, and you will be a blessing. I will bless those who bless you, and whoever curses you I will curse; and all peoples on earth will be blessed through you." So Abram left, as the LORD had told him. (Genesis 1:1–4)

Can you imagine? What would you do if God showed up to you tonight and told you to literally leave your family, the only home you knew, and wander around in the desert for an unforeseen amount of time? No coordinates, no map, nothing. They were to go to this unknown, unnamed land, and God would let them know when they got there. I can't even fathom the amount of faith it took, but we know that Abraham's response was to get up and go. It's later mentioned in Hebrews, "By faith Abraham, when called to go to a place he would later receive as his inheritance, obeyed and went, even though he did not know where he was going" (Hebrews 11:8).

What would stop you from getting up and going? Family? Friends? Maybe you are comfortable in the job you currently have, and perhaps the unknown in a shaky economy is more than you can handle. Jesus addressed this when He walked the earth and spoke truth to many who wanted to follow Him.

> As they were walking along the road, a man said to him, "I will follow you wherever you go." Jesus replied, "Foxes have holes and birds of the air have nests, but the Son of Man has no place to lay his head." He said to another man, "Follow me." But the man replied, "Lord, first let me go and bury my father." Jesus said to him, "Let the dead bury their own dead, but you go and proclaim the kingdom of God." Still another said, "I will follow you, Lord; but first let me go back and say good-by to my family." Jesus replied, "No one who puts his hand to the plow and looks back is fit for service in the kingdom of God." (Luke 9:57–62)

It is easy to follow Jesus when the circumstances are ironed out and every little detail is taken care of. But what about when things aren't quite as neat?

I was looking for work shortly after I got married, and despite the fact that I had a college degree, no one was hiring. I began volunteering for an organization that would later come to fruition as a full-time job. (I can now recognize this as the groundwork that God laid before me.) But where I was satisfied with that outcome, God was not and knew that I needed a challenge.

I took a two-week trip to Chad, Africa, providing a vacation Bible school to fifteen missionary kids. I met with their parents, heard their stories, and knew that there was change in my future. What was beginning to stir in my heart was the unknown. It involved leaving the salary, leaving the benefits, stepping out in faith, and trusting that God would meet all of my needs.

There wasn't anything set in stone; there were no rubrics for me to follow. It was God leading and me following, no matter where it took me.

Deuteronomy 5:32–33 says, "So be careful to do what the LORD your God has commanded you; do not turn aside to the right or to the left. Walk in all the way that the LORD your God has commanded you, so that you may live and prosper and prolong your days in the land that you will possess."

The end result of our lives is to give God glory. He has a plan already in place, and we just have to be willing to move forward and go after it. There is likely to be pain and heartache along the way, but those trials will help us grow and ultimately allow us to appreciate the experience that much more than if it had simply been given to us on a silver platter.

You may be thinking the same conversation that God and I have on a regular basis. "I'm not good enough. I mean seriously, God, have you seen me? Have you heard the thoughts that run through my head? I couldn't possibly—"

The really cool part about all of this is that God uses broken people to accomplish His work all the time. In fact, they are His favorites to use. If you honestly believe that you are too broken, you need to read your Bible more. Think about some of the most famous people in the Bible. Consider Noah for instance. When God looked at the world, Noah was the only one He found righteous. He was a drunk.

We've already talked about Abraham a couple times. You would think with his resume he would be pretty grounded. After all, we know him as the father of nations. But after God told him that he would be the father of the nations and have more heirs than grains of sand, he had faith in God despite his and his wife's ages only for a little while. Then he had an affair with his wife's servant to try to help the prophesy come to fruition.

Moses had to be a good guy, right? I mean, he helped the Israelites get out of Egypt. The Ten Commandments were given to him. Simply put, before God appeared to him in the desert, he had run away from Egypt as a murderer.

David, a man after God's own heart, was an adulterer, and he was responsible for a clear case of second-degree murder.

Solomon, the wisest man ever, had nine hundred wives and even more concubines. I think most people could tell you that being involved with that many women is asking for more drama than any man would ever want. Too bad Solomon didn't choose to be wise in that arena.

Not relating to the old men? All right, let's look at some of the lovely ladies in Jesus' lineage. Matthew lists five women in the lineage of Jesus. Historically this is extremely rare, as all lineages were traced through the men, but what is so incredible is the story of these women.

First is Tamar. Her story is found in Genesis 38. Basically she was originally the wife of Judah's oldest son, but he was evil, so God put him to death. Then she was supposed to have children with his brother to carry on the lineage; however, the little brother didn't like that idea and acted "wickedly," and so God also "put him to death." Then because Judah was worried that his youngest son might also succumb to the ill fate of his brothers, he told Tamar to "live as a widow in your father's house until my son Shelah grows up." Judah didn't intend to give Shelah to her as her husband (Genesis 38:14). So Tamar did what any desperate women would do in her situation. (I promise I'm being sarcastic here.) She dressed up like a prostitute and got her father-in-law to sleep with her so she could get pregnant. Awesome. However, God redeems. When Judah realized what had actually happened, he said "She is more righteous than I, since I wouldn't give her my son Shelah" (Genesis 38:26).

Next we have Rahab. If you know anything about Rahab, you know her title—prostitute. Her story is found in Joshua. In chapter 2, we learn that Joshua sent spies to look over the land they were about to enter, especially Jericho. When the spies entered Jericho, the king got word and came to find them. Lucky for them, Rahab hid them on her roof and spun a story to send the king in the wrong direction, giving the men a chance to escape. She had heard the stories of the great things God had done for these people and believed. When the Israelites came to Jericho, Joshua commanded the people, "Shout! For the LORD has given you the city ... Only Rahab the prostitute and all who are with her in her house shall be spared because she hid the spies we sent" (Joshua 6:16–17). It later says, "And she lives among the Israelites to this day" (Joshua 6:25).

Then we come to Ruth. Ruth even gets her own book in the Bible. In the four chapters we learn that she is first and foremost a Moabite. This story is set back in the time of the judges. It was dark and unforgiving times filled with much bloodshed. During this time there was a famine, and a couple decided to move to Moab with their two sons. While there, the sons married Moabite women, one of which was Ruth. While this wasn't forbidden, Deuteronomy 23:3 says that no Moabite was allowed to "enter the assembly of the LORD." Also while they were there, the father and both sons died. Tragic, yes, but you know God. He often works in mysterious ways. Naomi gave her daughter-in-laws an opportunity to stay in their homeland with their family, no strings attached. But Ruth would not leave her. Instead she said, "Where you go I will go, and where you stay I will stay. Your people will be my people and your God my God" (Ruth 1:16). Despite being an outsider, she managed to make an impression on Boaz, who later honored her and married her, bringing Ruth into the lineage of Jesus. She was the great grandmother of David.

Speaking of David, the next woman listed in the genealogy of Jesus is Bathsheba. Her story is found in 2 Samuel 11. While she is mentioned in the genealogy, she is mentioned as Uriah's wife but not by her own name. This lets you know right away that there is more to her story than simply being the mother of Solomon. King David was the great king of Israel, a man after God's own heart. But he still fell into sin. In this instance that sin was adultery (potentially rape) and murder. Bathsheba was bathing, and David happened to see her. Love at first sight? Probably not, but it was certainly a response to the lust that overcame him. David succumbed to his flesh, had her brought to him, and slept with her. Then the one-night-stand nightmare happened. She became pregnant. By law they could both be killed for this little *instance*, but instead David tried to manipulate the situation and *honor* her husband so that he might sleep with her and cover up her pregnancy. That doesn't work, so he places him on the front lines where he is sure to be killed. It works, and David takes Bathsheba as his wife. Only that's not the end. The prophet Nathan receives a word from God and confronts David about the entire situation. Once David confesses, there are still consequences to the sin. The child dies after only a short amount of time. Their firstborn who lived was to be the heir, Solomon, and become the king to finish the Lord's temple, and he is said to have been the richest and the wisest man to ever live.

Finally we have Mary, mother of Jesus. Mary was young, assumed to be only about fourteen or so years old and engaged to a man named Joseph. When she became pregnant, assumptions were made. After all, it *had* to be indiscretion. Joseph had every right, according to the law, to do anything from annulling the engagement to having her stoned. And instead God sent an angel to speak to Joseph, telling him the truth of the wonders that he was about to take part in. This would not be a normal (or acceptable) start to a marriage in that day and age, and yet it fulfilled the prophesy that the Savior would be born to a virgin. Mary's response is more mature than I could ever comprehend. Rather than complaining about the drastic inconvenience (and that's stating it lightly), she worshipped God and was humbled to be used in such an amazing way (Luke 1). She was not ignorant to the challenges ahead. Nor was she oblivious to the shame that may have resulted to not only her but her future child, who was the Christ.

The reality that we see today and see from the lives of those in the Bible is that God uses broken and imperfect people to accomplish His work. In the end God doesn't hold us accountable simply for doing good. No, He holds us accountable instead for doing what He asks us to do.

He realizes that we are going to mess it up. That's why He sent Jesus. It's not just that He died a death that we couldn't die. It's that He lived a life that was impossible for us to live so that we would be able to become representatives of God's love and grace to all the world. God is not simply to be studied but lived. He's not simply to be known but experienced. If you truly know God, then your life is to glorify Him.

Chapter 16 Review

Focus points

- God has a plan already in place, and we just have to be willing to move forward and go after it.
- God didn't choose perfect people to serve Him. He used those who were willing, broken and all.
- God doesn't hold us accountable simply for doing good, but He instead holds us accountable for doing what He asks us to do.
- God is to be lived, experienced, and ultimately glorified.

Taking a step over the starting line:

- Have you ever believed the lie that you weren't good enough for God to utilize?
- How can you be obedient to God even when your dreams don't go according to plan?

Chapter 17

Security in the Midst of Failure

Failure is a painful experience. I think that it is safe to assume that no one in his or her right mind has ever attempted something new with the *hope* of failing. We are talking about those new and wonderful adventures that are just standing on the horizon, tempting you to jump off the proverbial cliff into the vast unknown. But as painful as failure can be to us mentally, spiritually, and (depending on the situation) physically, it has its divine purpose.

We mentioned him briefly before, but let's look at Moses for a moment. From the beginning Moses got more than he could have hoped for, given his lineage. Not only did he escape a sure death after a decree from Pharaoh to kill all of the Hebrew sons of a certain age (with the obvious assistance of his beloved mother), but he is then raised in the palace as a prince with his own mother as the nurse. He is given an education and lives in luxury. But Moses made a drastic mistake that ended in the death of someone. He was now a murderer and had to run away. He finds himself in the middle of the desert, alone and afraid. At this point I think that it is safe to say that he saw himself as a failure.

Even the best circumstances do not guarantee a successful outcome. Moses had everything he could imagine from the beginning, and yet he still found himself lost and confused when all of the *stuff* that had been given to him and invested in him couldn't cover up the mistake of a murder.

But that is where God stepped in. Had Moses never failed as a prince of Egypt, he would not have ended up in the desert. Had he not ended up in the desert, he would not have encountered God in the burning bush. And had he not encountered God on that day, he would not have led the Hebrew slaves out of Egypt and to the Promised Land.

We focus so much on the details that we oftentimes miss the big picture. Moses had no way of knowing that he would find redemption in the God of his forefathers and become a man of faith and history. At the time of his failure, that was all he could see, and the possibility of something good coming out of something so wretchedly terrible was astronomically impossible at that point in time.

We also have a God who is in all ways omniscient and omnipotent. Imagine the most powerful being that you can possibly wrap your head around. Now add the ability to know absolutely everything—past, present, and future. That image that you have worked up doesn't even come close to matching who God is. He is greater than we can imagine. There is no way that we could ever understand Him in all of His intricacies. And the reality is that I wouldn't want to. Why would I want to worship a God I can understand? I would rather put my trust and faith in someone who knows everything and understands everything, *especially* the things that I do not.

When we try to accomplish things on my own, we are likely writing a recipe for disaster. We can only do so much alone. It is only when we cry out to God, "I can't do this without you!" At that moment we have just begun to further ourselves with the help and grace of Jesus.

The difference between feeling like a failure when we fail and simply failing is in faith. In Greek, faith can only be used as a verb. It has to have action behind it. Hebrews 11:1 defines it as "being sure of what we hope for and certain of what we do not see."

The word *sure* is from the Latin word *securus*, literally meaning without care. It's where we derive the word secure from. When we are sure of our hope, we are secure in that belief. There is no doubt or lingering questions about its absolute validity. Likewise, *certain* is to be established beyond doubt.

We do not need to see the physical being of God to have faith in Him. We know without a shadow of a doubt that He is in fact real. He has proven Himself over and over again in the lives of His people. We can believe what He says because He has proven Himself to be trustworthy. With that faith we can be sure that even when we fail, God has an incredible plan that can redeem us, even when we can't see it from our current circumstance.

In those moments we long to have a burning bush experience. We want to see God physically show Himself to us and tell us in an audible voice what our next step should be. In the days of the Bible, it feels as though God was visibly showing who He was constantly, so why doesn't He prove Himself through physical miracles that we can see today? In short, He does. Just not necessarily in the ways that you may anticipate.

We can't comprehend God, especially His power, and so we try to define Him in ways that our finite minds can understand. Unfortunately when we do this, we demean the great and arcane nature that is God. God's miracles and wonders are shown when they need to be shown.

We do not dictate the miracles that God produces. We simply ask, and that is a stumbling block. You might need to ask yourself, "Do I believe in God because of what God says or because of what I am seeing?"

"He'll be coming and going," he had said. "One day you'll see him and another you won't. He doesn't like being tied down—and of course he has other countries to attend to. It's quite all right. He'll often drop in. Only you mustn't press him. He's wild, you know. Not like a tame lion." (Lewis 1970)

Like the lion Aslan from The Chronicles of Narnia, God does not exist simply to grant us superfluous wishes and selfish desires.

God doesn't just do our bidding because we ask or demand it. God grants our desires because we have surrendered them to His plan. And if we get a no, it's because there is a greater good designed for us. We may not be able to see it, but that doesn't mean that it's not true.

All that we are, all that we do is to serve one ultimate purpose—to give God glory. Bringing Him glory through our lives with both successes and failures is the ultimate purpose. Paul was praying for the church of Ephesus and said in Ephesians 3:19 that he was praying specifically that they "know the love of Christ that surpasses knowledge, that you may be filled with all the fullness of God." We cannot know the love of Christ and be filled with the Spirit without it changing us. So how have those two factors changed who we are and where we can go?

In the same way that Paul was praying that they would know and truly understand the love of Christ, he was reminding them that they could also pray for help in that. The reality is that we are God's amazing and glorious design. He can and will help us because He designed us for that purpose. Ultimately prayer is simply about coming to God and submitting to Him and His will. It's not about the result, but rather it's allowing God to take us as a blank check and create the result that He desires. The results will be determined by how open-hearted we are to allow the Spirit of God to flow through and out of us. "God can do anything, you know—far more than you could ever imagine or guess or request in your wildest dreams! He does it not by pushing us around but by working within us, his Spirit deeply and gently within us" (Ephesians 3:20–22 MSG).

As we grasp that reality, it makes it easier to accept that we as believers reflect Jesus' unity and maturity when we step into our God-given reason and role. The sole reason, as I have said before, is to bring God glory. We do that through uniting Christ and His church. Our role is typically what we call our purpose. Jesus has given us our specific roles and responsibilities according to what is needed to bring Him that glory. The big question is this: Do we trust that God knows us better than we know ourselves? In other words, will we surrender everything, all of the details, all of the discrepancies that we think we need to fix, all of the challenges and seemingly impossible obstacles, every little thing? If we hang on to what we think is best, we will never get the opportunity to see what *God* says is best for us.

> And calling the crowd to him with his disciples, he said to them, "If anyone would come after me, let him deny himself and take up his cross and follow me. For whoever would save his life will lose it, but whoever loses his life for my sake and the gospel's will save it. For what does it profit a man to gain the whole world and forfeit his soul? For what can a man give in return for his soul?" (Mark 8:35–37)

Once we fully surrender to this reality, our failures can turn into successes. Once we cling to our faith despite our circumstances, we will see and hear the power of God working in and through our lives.

Chapter 17 Review

Focus points

- Failure can have a divine purpose.
- The difference between being a failure and simply failing is faith, and that faith in God is our security.
- God answers our desires when we have *completely* surrendered them to His plan (even if He answers with a no).
- We cannot know the love of Christ and be filled with the Spirit without it changing us.

Taking a step over the starting line

- Have there been *failures* in your life that God could redeem and use to bring Himself glory?
- Do you trust that God can in fact redeem those areas?
- Are you basing your faith in God on whether or not He answers your prayers in the way you want?

CHAPTER 18

The Finish Line

We must realize that we are all gifted and talented. We have been created to do so many amazing feats! Think about those who are gifted in healing. Doctors and nurses around the world save lives every day by being true to the gifts that they have been given. Or consider the people with the gift of music. I can't imagine a world without the beauty that a single voice or instrument can create and the emotions that it can stir. But ultimately with each gift and each dream of every person who has ever existed and ever will, we have been created to further God's kingdom. It's simply about using what you've been given to accomplish it.

We focus all of our energy on what we should do with our lives. We stress over which college we need to graduate from to get the internship that may (hopefully) lead to the job that will place us on the track that will get us the prestige ... and on and on and on. Instead what if we focused all of that same energy on working on our hearts? What if we took the same amount of time that we spend thinking about the perfect jobs and lives and devote it instead to serving and loving one another? When we work on our hearts and allow Jesus to change us from the inside out, what we do will just follow.

It needs to be about God's dream.

What is God's dream? Well, look back at the beginning.

> In the beginning God created the heavens and the earth. Now the earth was formless and empty, darkness was over the surface of the deep, and the Spirit of God was hovering over the waters. And God said, "Let there be light," and there was light. God saw that the light was good, and he separated the light from the darkness. God called the light "day," and the darkness he called "night." And there was evening, and there was morning—the first day. (Genesis 1:1–5)

On the first day God brought the heavens and the earth into existence, *and it was good*. It was perfect. Each new creation was *good and perfect*. This was the first step in God's dream—a place that was pristine and wonderful.

Try imagining your favorite place in the entire world. I know I said this earlier, but this is so important that it's worth saying again. Now close your eyes and take a moment to imagine it. Can you see it? Maybe you love the beach, so you are picturing a glassy, aqua ocean. You can hear it as the waves crash in its perfect rhythmic cadence against the warm, golden sand that you have squished between your toes. The radiant sun is beaming down and kissing your skin, not so hot that it burns but enough that you feel it warm you from the depths of your chest, reaching out to each individual finger and toe. There is a salty breeze that provides just enough movement to ward off the worst of the heat.

Perhaps you are more of a mountain lover. You see the vast expanse before you of tall, majestic peaks kissing the light blue sky. The smell of evergreen is like medicine to your soul, and the sounds of birds chirping, little critters rustling to find food, and fish jumping and splashing back into the water from a crystal lake is your idyllic perfection.

Now focus. The picture that you have created in your mind is nothing compared to what God had originally created. At this point it was *perfect*. Not a leaf out of place. The sun would never burn your skin. The plants would never leave a rash. Everything was intricately perfect beyond what we can even imagine. And that wasn't even His best work yet!

> Then God said, "Let us make man in our image, in our likeness, and let them rule over the fish of the sea and the birds of the air, over the livestock, over all the earth, and over all the creatures that move along the ground." So God created man in his own image, in the image of God he created him; male and female he created them. God blessed them and said to them, "Be fruitful and increase in number; fill the earth and subdue it. Rule over the fish of the sea and the birds of the air and over every living creature that moves on the ground." Then God said, "I give you every seed-bearing plant on the face of the whole earth and every

> tree that has fruit with seed in it. They will be yours for food. And to all the beasts of the earth and all the birds of the air and all the creatures that move on the ground—everything that has the breath of life in it--I give every green plant for food." And it was so. God saw all that he had made, and it was very good. And there was evening, and there was morning—the sixth day. (Genesis 1:26–31)

God's dream was not just this perfectly beautiful and wonderful world that He created. It was you! It was to live in harmony, in perfect company with you. That is why earth was created—for you. That's why we exist—to spend time with our Creator and to worship Him because He is worthy of our love and devotion every second of every day.

We focus on the tasks that we have to do. We get busy. We suddenly find ourselves in this whirlwind that we deem normal life, and we forget. We forget about the beginning. We forget the creation, the perfection. We forget what God had made just for us. But worse than forgetting the beginning, we forget the end.

> Then I saw a new heaven and a new earth, for the first heaven and the first earth had passed away, and there was no longer any sea. I saw the Holy City, the new Jerusalem, coming down out of heaven from God, prepared as a bride beautifully dressed for her husband. And I heard a loud voice from the throne saying, "Now the dwelling of God is with men, and he will live with them. They will be his people, and

God himself will be with them and be their God. He will wipe every tear from their eyes. There will be no more death or mourning or crying or pain, for the old order of things has passed away." He who was seated on the throne said, "I am making everything new!" Then he said, "Write this down, for these words are trustworthy and true." He said to me: "It is done. I am the Alpha and the Omega, the Beginning and the End. To him who is thirsty I will give to drink without cost from the spring of the water of life. He who overcomes will inherit all this, and I will be his God and he will be my son." (Revelation 21:1–7)

God created a brand-new heaven and earth for us! He takes away the pain that exists in the broken, sinful world we live in today, and He makes it perfect again. "I am making everything new!" Not just that, but the King of the universe is saying that if we give our lives to Him, not only will He be our God, but we will be His children.

Ephesians is an awesome book. Seriously it's one of those books that every time I read it, I find new nuggets of wisdom imbedded in the words. The more I lean in and search and ask, the more mysteries God reveals. After all, we're told, "Seek and you will find, knock and the door will be opened to you" (Matthew 7:7).

But here is the amazing part. Paul says what our purpose is in Ephesians. Yeah, I could have saved you some time and told you that at the beginning, but where's the fun in that?

Ephesians 4 says that we are called to "live a life worthy of the calling we have received" (Ephesians 4:1). Now if you only read this verse without reading the rest of the letter, it doesn't make *your calling* any clearer than mud. However, in Ephesians 2:10, he tells us that we are "God's handiwork, created in Christ Jesus to do good works, which God prepared in advance for us to do." That means that before time began, God tells us that "I Am." He always was, always is, and always will be. In that amazing truth we get to grapple with the reality that not only has God always been but that He has designed specific things in our lives for us to complete. In completing these good works, we bring God glory. Jesus was sent to pay the penalty of our sin to reconcile us to God (as Ephesians 2:14–16 indicates). God went to this extreme so that He could share His wisdom with each of us (Ephesians 3:10–11). All of those mysteries that confound us, we are told that God is going to reveal those wonders to us. We have the awesome opportunity to have the wisdom of the Creator shared with us for the distinct purpose of bringing us closer to Him. That is accomplished through the church—not through the established building that we meander into once a week but through each and every one of us as believers (Ephesians 2:22). When we believe and are baptized in the Holy Spirit, we can be filled with the "fullness of God" (Ephesians 3:17–20).

All of the tools that we are equipped with (gifts of the Spirit) are combined with the tools that He gives to other believers around us to essentially make an arsenal of awesome Holy Spirit power. But we aren't supposed to keep it to ourselves. We are equipped for the sole purpose of ... *service!* That's right. We go back to the service section. Paul words it a little more eloquently. He says that we are to "equip his people for works of service so that the body of Christ might be built up ... attaining to the whole measure of the fullness of Christ" (Ephesians 4:12–13). A pastor friend of mine would say, "Get it, live it, teach it." (Fielden 2012)

We are called to live in such a way that even the rulers and authorities will know the manifold wisdom of God (Ephesians 3:10). And then as we live it out in our own lives, we are to equip others to do the same. Every step of this process builds up the body of Christ. Every step brings God honor and glory beyond what anyone can imagine or comprehend.

That is the end. More so, that is the point. Our purpose cannot be separated from who we are in Christ because that *is* our purpose. What we do, how we use our gifts and talents, how exactly we serve—it all needs to be a reflection of Christ in us. Then and only then will we be able to get past the starting line and run the race as God has called us.

Chapter 18 Review

Focus points

- We need to adjust our dreams to line up with God's dream for us.
- We are God's dream.

- We are equipped through our gifts to serve and to train others to do the same.
- Our purpose in life is to reflect Christ in us through the manner in which we live.

Taking a step over the starting line

- What dreams do you need to surrender to God?
- What can you do to reflect Jesus in your everyday life?

Afterword

This is my heart written on the page and shared with you. I have tried to be honest with my testimony and helpful in my research, but the reality is that this race and this journey is one that I am still in the midst of, and thus, I am still figuring it out myself.

I pray that what I have shared and what God has revealed to me through these pages will touch your heart and thus change your life. Like I said at the beginning, I love books that inspire change. In the end it doesn't matter if you read one hundred books by the wisest men and women on the face of the earth if you don't get up and do something. So that is my challenge to each and every one of you. I challenge you to stop reading book after book and story after story about changing your life. I challenge you to stop setting aside the completed book and shrugging off any impact it may have made as you were reading its words. *Get up!* As Scripture says, *"Awake!"* (Ephesians 5). Get out into the world and be imitators of Christ. Get out into your world and serve and love others for no other reason than just because. Seek after God, ask Him questions, search His Word for answers, and trust Him when He reveals Himself to you.

I challenge you to run the race for if you run with the purpose and drive of the Holy Spirit, you will cross the finish line victoriously. There is no other option at that point. However, if you never get past the start, you will miss all of the wonders and awesome glory that awaits you during the race.

I don't often use The Message translation of the Bible, but I love how bluntly it words these verses. So I leave you with the same challenge I quoted in the dedication.

> Do you see what this means—all these pioneers who blazed the way, all these veterans cheering us on? It means we'd better get on with it. Strip down, start running—and never quit! No extra spiritual fat, no parasitic sins. Keep your eyes on Jesus, who both began and finished this race we're in. Study how he did it. Because he never lost sight of where he was headed—that exhilarating finish in and with God—he could put up with anything along the way: Cross, shame, whatever. And now he's there, in the place of honor, right alongside God. When you find yourselves flagging in your faith, go over that story again, item by item, that long litany of hostility he plowed through. That will shoot adrenaline into your souls! (Hebrews 12:1–3 MSG)

Bibliography

Batterson, Mark. *All In*. Grand Rapids: Zondervan, 2013.

Bureau of Labor Statistics, Department of Labor. Employee tenure. *The Editor's Desk*. Accessed on January 2010. Cited on April 10, 2014, http://www.bls.gov/opub/ted/2010/ted_20100927.htm.

—. Tenure down for men, up for women. *The Editor's Desk*. Accessed on June 29, 2001. Cited on April 10, 2014, http://www.bls.gov/opub/ted/2001/june/wk4/art05.htm.

Carter, Howard. *Questions and Answers on Spiritual Gifts*. Tulsa: Harrison House, 1991.

Chan, Francis. *Forgotten God*. Colorado Springs: David C. Cook, 2009.

Cook, Tony Bancroft and Barry. *Mulan*. Burbank: Walt Disney Video, 1998.

Cowen, Richard. "The Importance of Salt." *UC Davis Geology 115 course*. Accessed on April 21, 2014, http://mygeologypage.ucdavis.edu/cowen/~gel115/salt.html.

Feyjoo, Damien. (Student ministry leader) in discussion with the author, October 2013.

Fielden, Van. "Get it, Live it, Teach it" (sermon series, Vista Church, Orlando, FL, December 2012).

Forget, J. *The Catholic Encyclopedia*. New York: Robert Appleton Company, 1910.

Greenleaf, Robert K. *The Servant as Leader.* Westfield: Robert K. Greenleaf Center, 1982.

Groeschel, Craig. *WEIRD: Because Normal Isn't Working, Kindle Version.* Grand Rapids: Zondervan, 2011.

Hagin, Kenneth E. *The Gifts and Calling of God [Kindle Edition].* Broken Arrow: Faith Library Publications, 2011.

Houston, Joel. *From the Inside Out.* 2006 by Hillsong United.

Hudson, Hugh. *Chariots of Fire.* Torrance: Twentieth Century Fox Film Corporation, Allied Stars Ltd., Enigma Productions, 1981.

James Orr, MA, DD. Entry for "Eternal." *International Standard Bible Encyclopedia.* Accessed on April 19, 2014, http://www.biblestudytools.com/encyclopedias/isbe/eternal.html.

Keller, Dr. Tim. "Gifts and Talents." *The Resurgence.* Accessed in 2001, http://theresurgence.com/2012/11/08/gifts-and-talents.

Lewis, C. S. *Mere Christianity.* New York: Macmillian/Collier, 1952.

Lewis, C. S. *The Lion, the Witch, and the Wardrobe.* New York: Macmillan Publishing, Co., 1970.

Moore, Beth. *Believing God [Kindle Edition].* Nashville: B&H Publishing Group, 2004.

Newport, Frank. "Americans Continue to Believe in God." *Gallup, Inc.* Accessed on June 3, 2011. Cited on April 21, 2014, http://www.gallup.com/poll/147887/Americans-Continue-Believe-God.aspx.

Stanley, Andy. *The Principle of the Path.* Nashville: Thomas Nelson, 2008.

Stoppard, Tom. *The Real Thing.* London: [Faber and Faber], 1982.

Tozer, A. W. *The Pursuit of God (Special Kindle Format)*. Harrisburg: Christian Publications, Inc, 1948.

von Buseck, Craig. "Southern Baptists struggle with the Holy Spirit." *The Christian Broadcasting Network, Inc.* Accessed on April 5, 2014, http://www.cbn.com/spirituallife/churchandministry/vonbuseck_southern baptist_holyspirit.aspx.

"Would You Notice Your Own Family If They Were Homeless?" *Relevant Magazine*. Accessed on April 24, 2014, http://www.relevantmagazine.com/slices/social-experiment-would-you-notice-your-own-family-if-they-were-homeless.

About the Author

Becca earned her degree from the University of Florida and has spent the past five years delving into the wonderfully crazy world of ministry, developing a heart for mentoring high school- and college-aged girls. Born a proud fifth-generation Floridian, she loves all things Southern ranging from potlucks to pickup trucks, but she especially enjoys a cold glass of sweet tea. Following God's call to move their family, Becca currently resides in Fort Worth, Texas, with her husband and two daughters. You can read more from Becca at Simplylivingthelife.com.

CPSIA information can be obtained at www.ICGtesting.com
Printed in the USA
LVOW08s0929281114

415992LV00001B/3/P